D0754719

j976.4

Aylesworth, Thomas G.
    The Southwest: Colorado, New
Mexico, Texas.

DISCOVERING AMERICA

The Southwest

COLORADO • NEW MEXICO • TEXAS

By
Thomas G. Aylesworth
Virginia L. Aylesworth

CHELSEA HOUSE PUBLISHERS
New York • Philadelphia

3   5   7   9   8   6   4   2

Library of Congress Cataloging-in-Publication Data

Aylesworth, Thomas G.
   The Southwest: Colorado, New Mexico, Texas
Thomas G. Aylesworth, Virginia L. Aylesworth.
     p. cm.—(Discovering America)
   Includes bibliographical references and index.
   ISBN 0-7910-3412-7.
         0-7910-3430-5 (pbk.)
   1. Southwest, New—Juvenile literature. 2. Colorado—Juvenile literature. 3. Texas—Juvenile
literature. 4. New Mexico—Juvenile literature. [1. Southwest, New. 2. Colorado. 3. New
Mexico. 4. Texas.] I. Aylesworth, Virginia L. II. Title. III. Series: Aylesworth, Thomas G.
Discovering America.

F787.A95   1995   94-45786
976.4—dc20   CIP
                                            AC

CONTENTS

Colorado

    The state seal of Colorado was adopted in 1877. It is circular, and at top center is a triangle containing the "all-seeing" eye of God. Beneath are Roman fasces, or bound rods, representing power. Below is a shield bearing three mountains and a miner's pick and hammer. Beneath the shield is the state motto, and around the seal is printed "State of Colorado" and "1876," the year the state entered the Union.

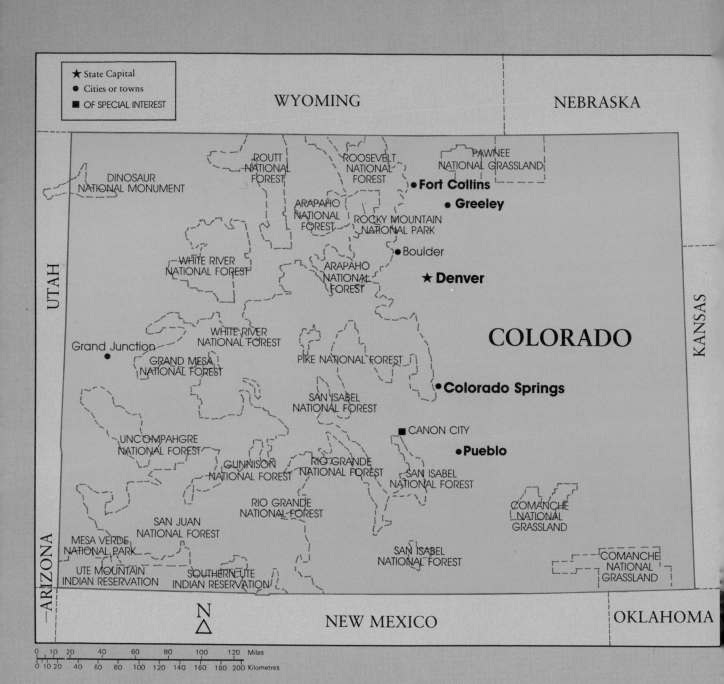

WYOMING

NEBRASKA

UTAH

KANSAS

ARIZONA

DINOSAUR
NATIONAL MONUMENT

ROUTT
NATIONAL
FOREST

ROOSEVELT
NATIONAL
FOREST

PAWNEE
NATIONAL GRASSLAND

● **Fort Collins**

ARAPAHO
NATIONAL
FOREST

● **Greeley**

ROCKY MOUNTAIN
NATIONAL PARK

WHITE RIVER
NATIONAL FOREST

ARAPAHO
NATIONAL
FOREST

● Boulder

★ **Denver**

COLORADO

Grand Junction
●

WHITE RIVER
NATIONAL FOREST

GRAND MESA
NATIONAL FOREST

PIKE NATIONAL FOREST

● **Colorado Springs**

SAN ISABEL
NATIONAL FOREST

UNCOMPAHGRE
NATIONAL FOREST

■ CANON CITY

● **Pueblo**

GUNNISON
NATIONAL FOREST

RIO GRANDE
NATIONAL FOREST

SAN ISABEL
NATIONAL FOREST

RIO GRANDE
NATIONAL FOREST

COMANCHE
NATIONAL
GRASSLAND

SAN JUAN
NATIONAL FOREST

MESA VERDE
NATIONAL PARK

SAN ISABEL
NATIONAL FOREST

COMANCHE
NATIONAL
GRASSLAND

UTE MOUNTAIN
INDIAN RESERVATION

SOUTHERN UTE
INDIAN RESERVATION

N
△

NEW MEXICO

OKLAHOMA

0 10 20   40   60   80   100   120   Miles
0 10 20 40   60   80 100 120 140 160 180 200 Kilometres

COLORADO
At a Glance

Capital: Denver

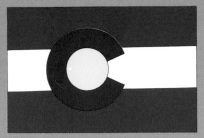

State Flag

State Flower:
Rocky Mountain
Columbine

State Bird:
Lark Bunting

Major Industries: Computer equipment,
food processing, aerospace, mining, livestock

Major Crops: Corn, wheat, hay, sugar beets

Size: 104,091 square miles (8th largest)
Population: 3,470,216 (26th largest)

7

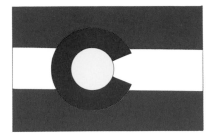

State Flag

The Colorado state flag, adopted in 1911, has three horizontal stripes of blue, white, and blue. On the left end of the flag is the letter "C" in red, encircling a golden disk, representing the state's gold production.

State Motto

Nil Sine Numine

This Latin phrase means "Nothing without Providence."

The Great Sand Dunes of Medano Peak are among the largest in the country and have been declared a national monument.

State Capital

Denver has been the capital of Colorado since 1867, nine years before it became a state.

State Name and Nicknames

In the beginning, a number of names were suggested for the Colorado Territory. Among them were Osage, Idaho, Jefferson, and Colona. But *Colorado,* Spanish for "colored red," was selected because it described the color of the Colorado River.

The most common nickname for Colorado is the *Centennial State* because it came into the Union 100 years after the signing of the Declaration of Independence. Because of its mountains, it is also known as the *Highest State* and the *Switzerland of America.*

State Flower

The Rocky Mountain columbine, *Columbine aquilegia caerulea,* was named the state flower in 1899.

State Tree

The state tree, although unofficial, is the blue spruce, *Picea pungens.*

State Bird

The lark bunting, *Calamospiza melancorys steineger,* was named the state bird in 1931.

State Animal

The Rocky Mountain bighorn sheep, *Ovis canadensis,* has been the state animal since 1961.

State Gem

Adopted in 1971, the aquamarine is the state gem.

State Song

"Where the Columbines Grow," by A. J. Flynn, was named the state song in 1915.

Population

The population of Colorado in 1992 was 3,470,216, making it the 26th most populous state. There are 31.65 people per square mile.

Industries

The principal industries in Colorado are tourism, manufacturing, government, agriculture, aerospace, and electronics equipment. In 1989, the state of Colorado earned $5.6 billion dollars from tourism.

Agriculture

The chief crops of the state are corn, wheat, hay, sugar beets, barley, potatoes, apples, peaches, pears, dry edible beans, sorghum, onions, and oats. Colorado is also a livestock state, and there are estimated to be some 2.8 million cattle, 220,000 hogs and pigs, 825,000 sheep, and 4 million chickens and turkeys on its farms. Oak, ponderosa pine, and Douglas fir trees are harvested. Gold, construction sand and gravel, and crushed stone are important mineral resources.

Government

The governor of Colorado is elected to a four-year term, as are the lieutenant governor, secretary of state, treasurer, and attorney general. The state legislature, or general assembly, which meets annually, contains a 35-member senate and a 65-member house of representatives. They are elected by separate legislative districts. Senators serve four-year terms and representatives serve two-year terms. The most recent state constitution was adopted in 1876. In addition to its two U.S. senators, Colorado has six representatives in the U.S. House of Representatives. The state has eight votes in the electoral college.

Sports

Sports are important in Colorado. The NCAA hockey championship has been won by the University of Denver (1958, 1960, 1961) and Colorado College (1950, 1957). The National Invitation Tournament basketball championship was won by the University of Colorado (1940), and the University of Colorado has won the

The skyline of Denver, or the "mile high city," is surrounded by a vast stretch of the Front Range.

Orange Bowl football game (1957, 1991).

On the professional level, the Denver Broncos of the National Football League play in Mile High Stadium, and the Denver Nuggets of the National Basketball Association play their games in McNichols Sports Arena.

Major Cities

Colorado Springs (population 281,140). Founded in 1871 by the Denver and Rio Grande Railroad as a summer resort,

the town lies at the foot of Pikes Peak. It is a beautifully maintained city, and has become a center of technology and culture.

Things to see in Colorado Springs: Pikes Peak, El Pomar Carriage House Museum, Broadmoor-Cheyenne Mountain Highway, Cheyenne Mountain Zoological Park, Shrine of the Sun, U.S. Air Force Academy, Pioneers' Museum, Colorado Springs Fine Arts Center, U.S. Olympic Training Complex, American Numismatic Association, McAllister House Museum (1873), Hall of Presidents, Pro Rodeo Hall of Fame and Museum of the American Cowboy, Pikes Peak Ghost Town, Old Colorado City, White House Ranch Historic Site, Flying W Ranch, May Natural History Museum, National Carvers Museum, Seven Falls, Palmer Park, Garden of the Gods, and Wildlife World Art Museum.

Denver (population 467,610). Settled in 1858, the capital city began as a gold miner's town. Today, Denver is a transportation, industrial, commercial, cultural, and vacation center.

Things to see in Denver:
State Capitol, Colorado History Museum, Denver Public Library, Denver Art Museum, Denver City and County Building, Greek Theater, United States Mint, Denver Center for the Performing Arts, Helen Bonfils Theatre Complex, Boettcher Concert Hall, Auditorium Theater (1905), Larimer Square, Sakura Square, Denver Firefighters Museum, Molly Brown House Museum (1889), Grant-Humphreys Mansion (1902), Pearce-McAllister Cottage (1899), Museum of Western Art, Forney Transportation Museum, Denver Children's Museum, Denver Museum of Natural History, Charles C. Gates Planetarium, Denver Zoo, Cheeseman Park, Denver Botanic Gardens, Elitch Gardens, and Chamberlin Observatory.

Places to Visit

The National Park Service maintains 21 areas in the state of Colorado: Black Canyon of the Gunnison National Monument, Colorado National Monument, Dinosaur National Monument, Florissant Fossil Beds National Monument, Great Sand Dunes National Monument, Hovenweep National Monument, Curecanti National Recreation Area, Mesa Verde National Park, Rocky Mountain National Park, Bent's Old Fort National Historic Site, Arapaho National Forest, Grand Mesa National Forest, Gunnison National Forest, Pike National Forest, Rio Grande National Forest, Roosevelt National Forest, Routt National Forest, San Isabel National Forest, San Juan National Forest, Uncompahgre National Forest, and White River

The restored buildings of Centennial Village in Greeley show how the area prospered during the late 19th century.

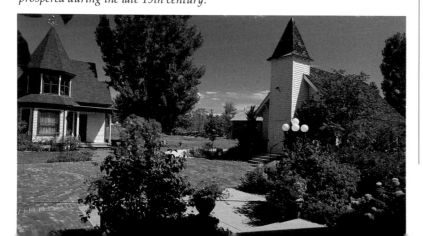

National Forest. In addition, there are 17 state recreation areas.

Aspen: Ashcroft Mining Camp. This preserved mining camp has buildings that date back to the 1880s.

Boulder: National Center for Atmospheric Research. Exhibits on atmospheric technology, the ozone layer, and windshear can be seen.

Burlington: Old Town. This is an historical Colorado pioneer village.

Cañon City: Buckskin Joe. This restored boom town features staged gunfights and coach rides.

Central City: Central Gold Mine and Museum. Mine tours are offered and the museum contains mining equipment.

Cripple Creek: Cripple Creek District Museum. Pioneer, mining, and railroad memorabilia are exhibited.

Dolores: Anasazi Heritage Center and Escalante Ruins. Here are artifacts from an Anasazi Indian village.

Durango: The Silverton. This railroad depot services the last regularly-scheduled narrow-gauge passenger train.

Estes Park: Enos Mills Cabin. Built in 1885, the cabin stands on a 200-acre nature preserve.

The varied rock formations at Cave of the Winds in Manitou Springs make it a popular tourist attraction.

Evergreen: Hiwan Homestead Museum. This 17-room Victorian log lodge was built in 1890.

Fairplay: South Park City Museum. This is a restored mining town with 30 original buildings.

Fort Collins: Fort Collins Museum. Among the exhibits is a model of the original fort.

Georgetown: Hotel de Paris Museum. This elaborately

decorated hotel was built in 1875.

Golden: Buffalo Bill Memorial Museum and Grave. The museum contains mementos of the famous scout.

Grand Junction: Dinosaur Valley Museum. The museum features animated models of dinosaurs.

Greeley: Centennial Village. Restored buildings, dating from 1860, can be toured.

Gunnison: Gunnison Pioneer Museum. Pioneer artifacts, a narrow-gauge railroad, and an old schoolhouse are exhibited.

Idaho Springs: Argo Town, USA. This reproduction of a western mining town contains a gold mill.

Leadville: Healy House-Dexter Cabin. Built in 1878, these buildings contain fine Victorian-era furnishings.

Manitou Springs: Cave of the Winds. A 40-minute guided tour features stalactites, stalagmites, and flowstone formations.

Montrose: Ute Indian Museum and Ouray Memorial Park. The museum is on the farm site of Chief Ouray.

Ouray: Box Cañon. The canyon is 20 feet wide and 400 feet deep.

Pueblo: Fred E. Weisbrod Aircraft Museum. This outdoor museum contains aircraft displays.

Steamboat Springs: Tread of Pioneer Museum. Pioneer, cattle ranching, and Indian artifacts are featured.

Sterling: Overland Trail Museum. Displays here include Indian memorabilia, a one-room schoolhouse, and a fire engine.

Trinidad: Baca House. Built in 1869, this nine-room adobe home was erected along the old Santa Fe Trail.

Vail: Colorado Ski Museum and Ski Hall of Fame. Skiing artifacts and photographs trace the history of skiing.

Events

There are many events and organizations that schedule activities of various kinds in the state of Colorado. Here are some of them.

Sports: Kinetic Conveyance Challenge (Boulder), Bolder Boulder (Boulder), Coors Classic International Bicycle Race (Boulder), Little Britches Rodeo (Burlington), Kit Carson County Fair and Rodeo (Burlington), Rodeo and Pioneer Celebration (Cañon City), Pikes Peak Auto Hill Climb (Colorado Springs), Broadmoor Invitational Men's and Women's Golf (Colorado Springs), Pikes Peak or Bust Rodeo (Colorado Springs), Ute Mountain Rodeo (Cortez), Hare and Hound Race (Craig), National Western Livestock Show, Horse Show and Rodeo (Denver), Arabian Horse Show (Estes Park), Horse Shows (Estes Park), Rodeo Weekend (Evergreen), World's Championship Pack Burro Race (Fairplay), Rodeo (Fort Morgan), Strawberry Days Festival and Rodeo (Glenwood Springs), Garfield County Fair and Rodeo (Glenwood Springs), World Footbag Association National Footbag Championship (Golden), Colorado Stampede (Grand Junction), Coors International Bicycle Classic (Grand Junction), Rocky Mountain Open Golf Tournament (Grand Junction), Sailing Regattas (Grand Lake), Turtle Races (Grand Lake), Independence Stampede Greeley Rodeo (Greeley), Cattlemen's Days, Rodeo and County Fair (Gunnison), Kids' Rodeo (La Junta), Boom Days and Burro Race (Leadville), Boulder County Fair and Rodeo (Longmont), Larimer County Fair and Rodeo (Loveland), Pikes Peak Marathon (Manitou Springs), Ski-Hi Stampede (Monte Vista), San Miguel Basin Fair and Rodeo (Norwood), Ouray County Fair and Rodeo (Ouray), Imogene

Pass Mountain Marathon (Ouray), Pueblo Motorsports Park (Pueblo), Arkansas River International White Water Boat Race (Salida), Iron Horse Race (Silverton), Hardrockers Holiday (Silverton), Rio Grande Raft Races (South Fork), Cowboys Roundup Rodeo (Steamboat Springs), Telluride Hang Gliding Festival (Telluride), Trinidad Roundup (Trinidad), Jerry Ford Invitational Golf Tournament and Concert (Vail), Coors Invitational Bicycle Classic (Vail), First Interstate Bank Cup (Winter Park).

Arts and Crafts: Summerfest Evergreen (Evergreen), North American Sculpture Exhibition (Golden), Rocky Mountain National Watermedia Exhibition (Golden), Artists' Alpine Holiday and Festival (Ouray), Culinary Arts Exhibit (Ouray).

Music: Aspen Music Festival (Aspen), Ballet/Aspen (Aspen), Colorado Music Festival (Boulder), Breckenridge Music Institute (Breckenridge), Blossom and Music Festival (Cañon City), Central City Jazz Festival (Central City), Central City Opera and Drama Festival (Central City), Colorado Springs Symphony (Colorado Springs), Indian Dances (Cortez), Denver Symphony (Denver), Central City Opera (Denver), Opera Colorado (Denver), Music in the

The Telluride Bluegrass Festival offers country music in a breathtaking setting.

Mountains (Estes Park), Music in Ouray (Ouray), Pueblo Symphony (Pueblo), Brass Band Festival (Silverton), Bluegrass Festival (Telluride), Jazz Festival (Telluride), Chamber Music Festival (Telluride), Winter Park Jazz Festival (Winter Park).
Entertainment: Sunshine Festival (Alamosa), Winterskol Carnival (Aspen), Banana Season (Aspen), Winter Carnival (Breckenridge), No Man's Land Day Celebration (Breckenridge), Madam Lou Bunch Day (Central City), Montezuma County Fair (Cortez), Harvest Festival Celebration (Cortez), Flauschink (Crested Butte), Donkey Derby Days (Cripple Creek), Deltarado Days (Delta), Cherry Blossom

The lake reflects the crowds who come to hear the music at the Winter Park Jazz Festival.

The United States Air Force Academy, near Colorado Springs.

Festival (Denver), Snowdown Winter Carnival (Durango), Durango Fiesta Days (Durango), La Plata County Fair (Durango), Colorfest (Durango), Trail Ridge Road Opening (Estes Park), Aspenfest (Estes Park), Rooftop Rodeo (Estes Park), Mountain Rendezvous (Evergreen), Fasching (Georgetown), Christmas Market Weeks (Georgetown), Buffalo Bill Days (Golden), Winter Carnival (Grand Lake), Buffalo Barbecue (Grand Lake), Weld County Fair (Greeley), Gold Rush Days (Idaho Springs), Arkansas Valley Fair and Exposition (La Junta), Early Settlers Day (La Junta), Winter Carnival (Lake City), Alfred Packer Day (Lake City), Winter Carnival (Leadville), Oro City: "Rebirth of a Miners' Camp" (Leadville), Stone Age Fair (Loveland), Good Old Days Celebration (Lyons), San Luis Valley Fair (Monte Vista), Pioneer Day (Norwood), Winter Fest (Pagosa Springs), Colorado State Fair (Pueblo), Chaffee County Fair (Salida), Annual Rhubarb Festival (Silverton), Winter Carnival (Steamboat Springs), Logan County Fair (Sterling), Sugar Beet Days (Sterling), Wine Festival and Balloon Rally (Telluride), Vail America Days (Vail), Vailfest (Vail), Will Overhead Day (Walsenburg), Winter Wild West Week (Winter Park), Springsplash (Winter Park).

Tours: Victorian Christmas and Home Tour (Leadville), Colorfest (Telluride), River Rendezvous (Telluride).

Theater: Colorado Shakespeare Festival (Boulder), Imperial Players (Cripple Creek), Thunder Mountain Lives Tonight! (Delta), The Denver Center for the Performing Arts (Denver), The Helen Bonfils Theatre Complex (Denver), Auditorium Theater (Denver), Diamond Circle Theatre (Durango), Barleen Family Theater (Estes Park), Players Company—Pine Cone Theater (Grand Lake), Koshare Winter Night Ceremonial (La Junta), Snowmass/Aspen Repertory Theatre (Snowmass Village), Creede Repertory Theater (South Fork), Balcony Theatre (Winter Park).

Cattle graze in a lush field as the Rocky Mountains loom in the distance.

The Land and the Climate

Colorado is bordered on the west by Utah, on the north by Wyoming and Nebraska, on the east by Nebraska and Kansas, and on the south by New Mexico and Oklahoma. There are four major land regions in the state: the Colorado Plateau, the Intermontane Basin, the Rocky Mountains, and the Great Plains.

The Colorado Plateau lies along most of the western border, from north to south. It covers almost one-fifth of the state, and is a region of high hills, plateaus, deep valleys, and mesas—flat-topped hills with steep sides. The mesas support cattle and sheep ranches, and in the valleys farmers raise fruit, hay, beans, and vegetables. The region is rich in mineral resources, including oil and natural gas, uranium, copper, zinc, lead, and silver.

The Intermontane Basin is north of the Colorado Plateau on the state's northern border. As its name suggests, it lies between two mountainous regions of the Rockies. Forested hills and sagebrush plateaus form the landscape. Sheep ranches dot the plateaus, and oats and beans are raised here. There is also some coal mining.

The Rocky Mountains occupy central Colorado and a small area at the northwest corner of the state. The Colorado Rockies have been called the "Roof of North America," since more than 50 of their peaks rise 14,000 feet or more above sea level. They are the tallest in the entire Rocky Mountain chain, which extends from Alaska to Mexico. This is a region of forests and forest products, with some hay, oat, and vegetable crops. Extensive mining is carried out: lead, copper, tungsten, beryllium, sand, gravel, molybdenum, silver, and gold are found here. The Continental Divide runs through the Colorado Rockies. Streams east of it flow into the Atlantic Ocean, while those west of it run to the Pacific.

The Great Plains cover the eastern two-fifths of the state and are part of the vast interior plain that extends from Canada to Mexico.

The cool waters of Bear Lake lie at the base of Hallett Peak in Colorado's Rocky Mountain National Park.

The 14,143-foot peak of Mt. Sneffels frames the Dallas Valley near Ouray.

The land slopes from east to west to the foothills of the Rocky Mountains. Irrigation has made it possible to farm the region, and to pasture beef and dairy cattle. Crops raised here include sugar beets, potatoes, barley, corn, wheat, hay, rye, and sorghum.

Colorado is the source of more important rivers than any other state. Rivers that rise here include the Arkansas, North and South Platte, Republican, Rio Grande, Colorado, Gunnison, and San Juan. Many lakes are found in the mountains, including Grand Lake, the state's largest natural lake, which covers about 600 acres.

The mountainous western sections of Colorado are generally cooler than the plains. Because of great differences in altitude within short distances, temperatures and weather conditions can change rapidly as one travels through the state. In Colorado, as in Montana, a *chinook*, or warm wind, often blows down the eastern slopes, raising winter temperatures 20 or more degrees Fahrenheit. In the plains, Burlington has an average January temperature of 28 degrees F. and a July average of 74 degrees F. Leadville, in the mountains, has a January average of 18 degrees F., while its July average is 55 degrees F. The state's precipitation is some 15 inches per year, with most rain and snow falling on the western slopes of the mountains.

The History

Cliff dwellings almost a thousand years old at Mesa Verde are all that remains of the Pueblo-type Anasazi culture that flourished in Colorado between A.D. 750 and 1300. By the time Spanish explorers arrived, the region was inhabited primarily by nomadic Plains Indians, including the Arapaho, Cheyenne, Comanche, Kiowa, and Pawnee. The Utes lived in the mountain valleys.

The Spaniards who came to what is now Colorado about 1541 were looking for gold. When they failed to find it, they returned to Mexico, leaving no settlements. In 1682 the French explorer Robert Cavelier, known as La Salle, claimed part of the eastern region for his country when he asserted dominion over the vast territory he called Louisiana. The Spanish returned in 1706, when Juan de Ulibarri claimed the territory for Spain.

Most of present-day Colorado became part of the United States in 1803, with the Louisiana Purchase from France, which sold its territories west of the Mississippi to the young United States. Zebulon M. Pike, an army officer and explorer, entered the Colorado region on a surveying trip in 1806. In his report he described the steep mountain that was named for him—Pikes Peak.

Pike was followed in 1820 by another exploration party under the leadership of army officer Stephen H. Long. Thirteen years later, the first permanent American settlement in the region, Bent's Fort, was set up by the Bent and St. Vrain Fur Company near the present site of La Junta. Kit Carson and other frontiersmen used it as a base.

When Mexico claimed its independence from Spain in 1821, the part of western Colorado that was still under Spanish rule became Mexican territory. The United States and Mexico went to war for title to the Southwest and California in 1846, and a million square miles of territory, including western Colorado, were acquired in 1848, when Mexico was defeated.

Mesa Verde, in the southwestern part of the state, was the home of prehistoric Indians who built elaborate cliff dwellings.

When gold was discovered along Cherry Creek in 1858, a stream of prospectors poured into the area that is now Denver. Rich strikes the following year brought fresh wagon trains filled with gold seekers: their slogan was "Pikes Peak or Bust." By the end of 1859, some 100,000 people had come to Colorado. Silver was discovered soon afterward, and additional prospectors arrived. Mining camps, most of them crude tent cities clinging to the rugged slopes of the Rockies, sprang up to become part of Colorado's colorful, robust history.

Newcomers to Colorado ignored both Indian rights to the land and U.S. government treaties that had promised to respect those rights. They set up what they called the Jefferson Territory, which the government refused to recognize. Finally, Congress created the Colorado Territory in 1861, and the U.S. Army waged war on the Colorado Indians for the rest of the decade. In 1864 Colorado militia

Denver, the "Queen City of the Plains," and the capital of the state of Colorado was founded by prospectors in 1859.

led by Colonel John M. Chivington attacked peaceful Cheyenne and Arapaho villagers at Sand Creek and killed hundreds of men, women, and children in what became known as the Sand Creek Massacre. It was one of the darkest chapters in American history. The United States government admitted responsibility for the tragedy and awarded the Indians some compensation for their losses. In 1868 a large force of Indians attacked 50 U.S. Army scouts near the Arikaree River in eastern Colorado. The resulting battle lasted for days before fresh troops rescued the soldiers.

The Meeker Massacre of 1879 was the last major combat between Indian and government forces in Colorado. Indian agent Nathan C. Meeker, who tried to make small farmers of the Utes on unsuitable reservation land, was killed during an uprising, and the U.S. Army moved in to quell the riot. The venerable Ute chief Ouray intervened to restore order.

Railroads reached Colorado in 1870, when the Denver Pacific linked Denver with the main line of the Union Pacific at Cheyenne, Wyoming. That same year the Kansas Pacific completed a line to Denver, and Colorado was tied to the East Coast. Irrigation systems were developed in eastern Colorado to open the vast plains to profitable agriculture.

Colorado claimed its nickname as the Centennial State when it was admitted to the Union in 1876, just 100 years after the signing of the Declaration of Independence. Territorial governor John L. Routt was elected the first governor of the nation's 38th state.

The discovery of gold in the Rocky Mountains in 1858 brought prospectors and settlers to the Colorado Territory.

In 1893, when business was in a nationwide decline, the federal government cancelled its agreement to buy large quantities of Colorado silver. The mining towns of Leadville and Aspen were severely affected, but Robert Womack's major gold strike at Cripple Creek helped revitalize the mining industry. (Later Leadville was restored as a tourist attraction and Aspen became a popular ski resort.)

In 1902 construction began on the railroad that would cross the mountains to the West Coast, and by 1910 Colorado had almost 800,000 residents. Oil had been discovered in the 1860s, but it did not become a major industry until the automobile was developed at the turn of the century. This new form of transportation also made Colorado a popular vacation and recreation center.

During the 1940s, Colorado's economy and population kept growing. When the United States entered World War II, in 1941, the government established several military bases in the state. Wartime demands for defense and consumer goods kept employment high in the mining and petroleum fields. The postwar selection of Colorado Springs as the site of the new United States Air Force Academy, and installation of major peacetime military bases, brought continued growth. New dams and reservoirs were built, and the Alva B. Adams Tunnel carried water through the mountains to formerly arid eastern farmlands.

By 1954, manufacturing replaced agriculture as the state's leading industry. The mining and milling of uranium and the manufacture of electronic parts have also become important industries. In the 1970s, energy companies expanded operations to explore Colorado's resources of coal, natural gas, petroleum, and oil shale. Today Colorado's economy is recovering from the economic difficulties that affected most of the nation in the mid-1980s. In addition, pollution, urban decay, and overcrowding on the edge of the Rocky Mountains are problems which Coloradans are currently trying to solve.

Today manufacturing, mining, and tourism all contribute to Colorado's prosperity, and new residents arrive every year, attracted by the beauty and diversity of the "highest state."

Education

The first school in Colorado was established near Denver in 1859 to teach the children of gold miners. By 1862 many other towns had their own public schools. The first public library in Colorado opened in 1860, and a year later the region's first institution of higher education, the University of Colorado, was founded at Boulder. By the time Colorado became a state, four other colleges and universities were operating: the University of Denver (1864), Colorado State University (1870), Colorado College (1874), and the Colorado School of Mines (1874).

Heavyweight champion Jack Dempsey, born in Manassa, Colorado, works out at Stillman's Gym in New York, in 1920.

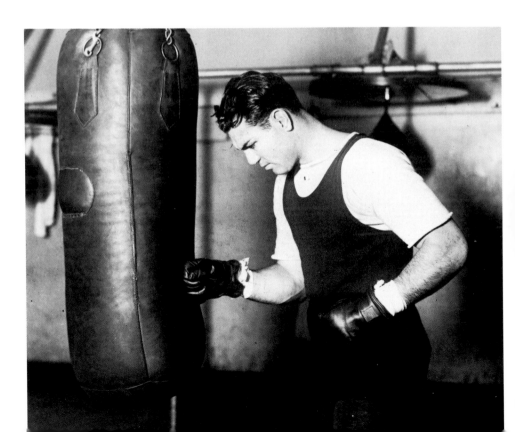

Astronaut Scott Carpenter, a native of Boulder, speaks to President Kennedy after his successful orbital flight in 1962.

The People

More than 80 percent of the people in Colorado live in metropolitan areas such as Denver, Colorado Springs, and Boulder. Approximately 95 percent of Colorado residents were born in the United States. Although most Coloradans are Protestants, the Roman Catholic Church is the largest single religious group. Major Protestant denominations include the Baptist, Methodist, Presbyterian, and United Church of Christ.

Famous People

Many famous people were born in the state of Colorado. Here are a few:

Ward Bond 1903-60, Denver. Film actor: *My Darling Clementine, Rio Bravo*

Scott Carpenter b. 1925, Boulder. Astronaut

Lon Chaney 1883-1930, Colorado Springs. Film actor: *The Phantom of the Opera, The Hunchback of Notre Dame*

Jack Dempsey 1895-1983, Manassa. Heavyweight boxing champion

Douglas Fairbanks 1883-1939, Denver. Film actor: *The Mark of Zorro, Robin Hood*

Pat Hingle b. 1923, Denver. Stage and film actor: *On the Waterfront, Norma Rae*

Shirley Hufstedler b. 1925, Denver. First secretary of education

Ken Kesey b. 1935, La Junta. Novelist: *One Flew Over the Cuckoo's Nest, Garage Sale*

Willard Libby b. 1908, Grand Valley. Nobel Prize-winning chemist

Edward L. Tatum 1909-75, Boulder. Nobel Prize-winning biochemist

Byron R. White b. 1917, Fort Collins. Supreme Court justice

Colleges and Universities

There are many colleges and universities in Colorado. Here are the more prominent, with their locations, dates of founding, and enrollments.

Adams State College of Colorado, Alamosa, 1921, 2,125

Colorado College, Colorado Springs, 1874, 1,903

Colorado School of Mines, Golden, 1874, 1,991

Colorado State University, Fort Collins, 1870, 17,572

Colorado Technical College, Colorado Springs, 1965, 1,244

Fort Lewis College, Durango, 1911, 4,096

Regis University, Denver, 1877, 1,161

United States Air Force Academy, Colorado Springs, 1954, 4,000

University of Colorado at Boulder, 1876, 20,043; *at Colorado Springs*, 1965, 5,751; *at Denver*, 1912, 6,128

University of Denver, Denver, 1864, 2,686

Western State College of Colorado, Gunnison, 1901, 2,668

Where To Get More Information

Division of Commerce and Development
State Office of Tourism
1313 Sherman Street
Denver, CO 80203
or call, 1-800-433-2656

New Mexico

The state seal of New Mexico, adopted in 1913, is circular. On it are two eagles representing the annexation of New Mexico by the United States. The Mexican eagle has a snake in its beak and cactus in its talons. The American bald eagle, with arrows in its talons, is shielding the Mexican eagle with outstretched wings. Under the eagles is a scroll bearing the state motto. Around the edge is printed "Great Seal of the State of New Mexico" and "1912," the year of the state's admission to the Union.

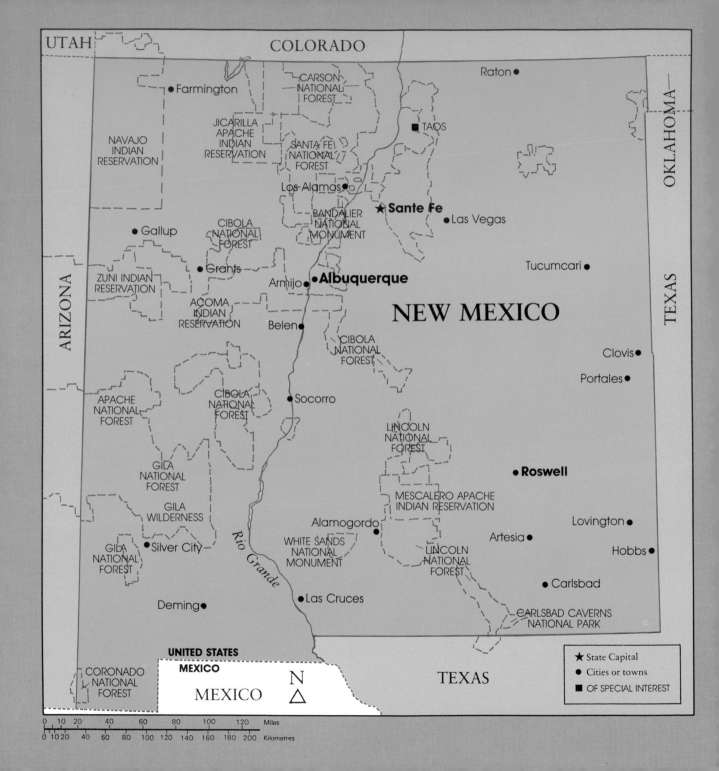

UTAH   COLORADO

OKLAHOMA

●Raton

ARIZONA

●Farmington

CARSON
NATIONAL
FOREST

NAVAJO
INDIAN
RESERVATION

JICARILLA
APACHE
INDIAN
RESERVATION

SANTA FE
NATIONAL
FOREST

■ TAOS

Los Alamos●

★ **Sante Fe**

●Las Vegas

●Gallup

CIBOLA
NATIONAL
FOREST

BANDALIER
NATIONAL
MONUMENT

●Grants

ZUNI INDIAN
RESERVATION

Armijo ● ●**Albuquerque**

Tucumcari●

NEW MEXICO

ACOMA
INDIAN
RESERVATION

Belen ●

CIBOLA
NATIONAL
FOREST

Clovis●

Portales●

APACHE
NATIONAL
FOREST

CIBOLA
NATIONAL
FOREST

● Socorro

LINCOLN
NATIONAL
FOREST

GILA
NATIONAL
FOREST

● **Roswell**

MESCALERO APACHE
INDIAN RESERVATION

GILA
WILDERNESS

Lovington ●

Alamogordo●

GILA
NATIONAL
FOREST

●Silver City

WHITE SANDS
NATIONAL
MONUMENT

Artesia ●

Hobbs ●

LINCOLN
NATIONAL
FOREST

Deming●

Rio Grande

● Las Cruces

● Carlsbad

CARLSBAD CAVERNS
NATIONAL PARK

UNITED STATES

MEXICO

N

★ State Capital

MEXICO

△

● Cities or towns

TEXAS

■ OF SPECIAL INTEREST

0	10	20		40		60		80		100		120		Miles
0	10 20		40		60	80		100	120		140	160	180	200	Kilometres

CORONADO
NATIONAL
FOREST

NEW MEXICO

At a Glance

Capital: Santa Fe

State Flower:
Yucca

State Bird:
Roadrunner

State Flag

Major Crops: Wheat, hay, sorghum, cotton

Major Industries: Electrical machinery, agriculture, mining

Size: 121,593 square miles (5th largest)
Population: 1,581,227 (37th largest)

State Flag

Adopted in 1925, the state flag is yellow; in the center, in red, is the ancient sun symbol of the Zia Pueblo Indians. The red and yellow colors represent the Spanish flag, recalling the fact that New Mexico was once Spanish territory.

State Salute to the Flag

In 1953, the state legislature adopted a salute to the state flag, written both in English and Spanish, reading: "I salute the flag of the state of New Mexico, the Zia symbol of perfect friendship among united cultures."

State Motto

Crescit Eundo

Adopted in 1851, this Latin motto means "It grows as it goes."

State Slogan

In 1975, a state slogan was designated: "Everybody Is Somebody in New Mexico."

The upper river flows through the Rio Grande Gorge near Taos.

State Capital

San Gabriel was the capital of New Mexico from 1599 to 1610, and Santa Fe has been the capital since then.

State Name and Nicknames

The land that was to become New Mexico was named Nuevo Mexico in 1561 by Fray Jacinto de San Francisco. The word *Mexico* in the Aztec language meant "Place of Mexitli"—one of the Aztec war gods. When the territory was taken over by the United States, Nuevo Mexico became New Mexico.

New Mexico is known as the *Land of Enchantment* because of its beauty and rich history. It is also referred to as the *Cactus State* because the plants are so numerous there.

State Flower

The yucca flower, *Yucca aloifolia*, was selected as the state flower in 1927, after a vote by school children and the endorsement of the First Federation of Women's Clubs.

State Tree

Pinus edulis, the nut pine (or piñon), was named the state tree in 1948.

State Bird

The roadrunner, *Geococcyx californianus*, has been the state bird of New Mexico since 1949. It also has another name—the chaparral bird.

State Animal

Selected in 1963, the state animal is the New Mexico black bear, *Euarctos americanus*.

State Fish

The New Mexico cutthroat trout, family *Salmonidae*, was adopted as state fish in 1955.

State Fossil

Coelophysis was named the state fossil in 1981.

State Gem

Selected in 1967, the state gem is the turquoise.

State Grass

The blue grama grass, *Bouteloua gracillis*, was named state grass in 1973.

State Vegetables

The state vegetables, selected in 1965, are the pinto bean and the chili.

State Songs

New Mexico has two state songs, one in English and one in Spanish. The English song, "O, Fair New Mexico," words and music by Elizabeth Garrett, was adopted in 1917. The Spanish language state song, "Asi Es Nuevo Méjico," words and music by Amadeo Lucero, was adopted in 1971.

Population

The population of New Mexico in 1992 was 1,581,227, making it the 37th most populous state. There are 12.46 people per square mile.

Industries

The principal industries of the state are extractive industries, tourism, and agriculture. The chief

Alamo Canyon in Bandelier is a national monument. Some canyons in this area contain the homes of the Pueblo peoples.

manufactured products are foods, electrical machinery, apparel, lumber, printing, and transportation equipment.

Agriculture

The chief crops of the state are wheat, hay, sorghum, grain, onions, cotton, and corn. New Mexico is also a livestock state, and there are estimated to be some 1.34 million cattle, 27,000 hogs, 462,000 sheep, and 1.43 million chickens and turkeys on its farms. Ponderosa pine and Douglas fir trees are harvested. Copper, potash, construction sand and gravel are important mineral resources.

Government

The governor of New Mexico is elected to a four-year term, as are the lieutenant governor, secretary of state, auditor, treasurer, attorney general, and commissioner of public lands. The state legislature, which meets annually, consists of a 42-member senate and a 70-member house of representatives. Senators are elected to four-year terms and representatives to two-year terms. Voters elect one senator from each senatorial district and one representative from each representative district. The most recent state constitution was adopted in 1911. In addition to its two U.S. senators, New Mexico has three representatives in the House of Representatives. The state has five votes in the electoral college.

Sports

Sporting events at all levels are held throughout the state. In 1956, the Little League World Series was won by Roswell.

Albuquerque, on the Rio Grande River, is known for its clean air and the influence of Native American culture on the desert community.

Major Cities

Albuquerque (population 384,619). Founded in 1706, the city was named after the Duke of Alburquerque, who was viceroy of New Spain (the first "r" was dropped from the name). The largest city in New Mexico, its pleasant climate has made it famous as a health center. The Old Town section was founded in 1706 as a way station on the Old Chihuahua Trail, also known as the Camino Real (Royal Way).

Albuquerque grew after World War II with the coming of the Nuclear Age. The Atomic Energy Commission began nuclear weapon's projects at Sandia base and Kirtland Air Force Base. Today, Albuquerque, surrounded by mountains, is bustling and growing and is popular among tourists.

Things to see in Albuquerque: Old Town, Maxwell Museum of Anthropology, Museum of Geology and Meteoritics, Jonson Gallery, Thompson Gallery, Fine Arts Center, Rio Grande Nature Center, Albuquerque Museum, New Mexico Museum of Natural History, Telephone Pioneer Museum, Indian Pueblo Cultural Center, National Atomic Museum, the Rio Grande Zoological Park, Isleta Pueblo, Indian Petroglyph State Park, Coronado State Monument, and Sandia Peak Aerial Tramway.

Santa Fe (population 56,537). Founded in 1610 by Pedrode Peralta, the third Spanish governor of the province of New Mexico, on the ruins of an Indian settlement. The Pueblo Indians revolted in 1680 and drove the Spanish from Santa Fe. The Spaniards regained control in 1692, and in 1846 the United States conquered the area from Mexico. The capital city is located at the base of the Sangre de Cristo Mountains. Its location, 7,000 feet above sea level, accounts for its cool and bracing climate. It is in the center of Pueblo Indian country and has a strong Mexican flavor.

The Plaza lies at the end of the Sante Fe trail in the historic section of the city.

Both English and Spanish are spoken here and it is a popular tourist resort.

Things to see in Santa Fe:
The Plaza, Palace of the Governors, Museum of Fine Arts, Federal Court House, Scottish Rite Temple, Sena Plaza, Prince Plaza, Cathedral of St. Francis (1869), La Fonda Hotel, Loretto Chapel, Famous Staircase, Footsteps Across New Mexico, San Miguel Mission, Oldest House, State Capitol, St. Francis School, Canyon Road, Cristo Rey Church, Camino del Monte Sol, Museum of Indian Arts and Culture, Museum of International Folk Art, Wheelwright Museum, Santuario de Guadalupe (about 1785), Old Cienega Village Museum, Institute of American Indian Arts Museum, and San Ildefonso Pueblo.

Places to Visit

The National Park Service maintains 17 areas in the state of New Mexico: Carlsbad Caverns National Park, Chaco Culture National Historic Park, El Morro National Monument, Bandelier National Monument, Salinas Pueblo Missions National Monument, White Sands National Monument, Aztec Ruins National Monument, Capulin Mountain National Monument, Fort Union National Monument, Pecos National Monument, Gila Cliff Dwellings National Monument, Malpais National Monument and National Conservation Area, Carson National Forest, Cibola National Forest, Gila National Forest, Lincoln National Forest, and Santa Fe National Forest. In addition, there are 38 state recreation areas.

Alamogordo: International Space Hall of Fame. This museum contains spacecraft and equipment.

Artesia: First Underground School in the U.S. The school, whose roof is at ground level, was built for protection from radioactive fallout.

Carlsbad: Living Desert State Park. This indoor/outdoor living museum has a large cactus collection and native animals.

Chama: Cumbres and Toltec Scenic Railroad, New Mexico Express. Visitors can make excursions aboard an 1880s narrow-gauge steam train.

Cimarron: Philmont Scout Ranch. This 138,000-acre camp also includes the Kit Carson Museum, Ernest Thompson Seton Memorial Library, and Philmont Museum.

Cloudcroft: Sacramento Mountains Pioneer Village. Exhibits show 1880-1910 mountain life.

Columbus: Columbus Historical Museum. This museum, in a 1902 railroad station, has exhibits of the 1916 raid on the town by the Mexican bandit Pancho Villa.

Dulce: Jicarilla Apache Indian Reservation. Descendents of the Indian tribe live here.

Española: Ghost Ranch Living Museum. Animals native to the area can be seen here.

Hobbs: Confederate Air Force Flying Museum. World War II aircraft are displayed.

Las Cruces: Mesilla. This is the historic village where the Gadsden Purchase was signed.

Las Vegas: Theodore Roosevelt Rough Riders' Memorial and City Museum. Mementos of the cavalry unit are exhibited.

Los Alamos: Bradbury Science Museum of the Los Alamos National Laboratory. Exhibits on the history of the atomic bomb and other nuclear weapons are featured.

Mescalero: Mescalero Apache Reservation. About 2,400 Indians live on this beautiful reservation.

Raton: Folsom Museum. The museum contains the remains of Folsom Man, a race that lived here about 12,000 B.C.

Roswell: Roswell Museum and Art Center. The museum contains the workshop of Dr. Robert H. Goddard, the Father of Rocketry.

Ruidoso: Old Dowlin Mill. This mill is over 100 years old.

Silver City: Piños Altos. This is a ghost town.

Socorro: Old San Miguel Mission. This is a restoration of the 1598 mission.

Taos: Kit Carson Home and Museum. Built in 1825, this was the home of the famous scout.

Kit Carson's home in Taos is open to visitors. The famous frontiersman purchased the abobe dwelling in 1843 at the time of his marriage to Josefa Jaranillo.

Events

There are many events and organizations that schedule activities of various kinds in the state of New Mexico. Here are some of them.

Sports: Indian National Finals Rodeo (Albuquerque), Smokey Bear Stampede (Capitán), Maverick Club Rodeo (Cimarron), Pioneer Days and PRCA Rodeo (Clovis), Clovis Balloon Fiesta (Clovis), Great American Duck Race (Deming), All-Indian Rodeo (Dulce), Little Beaver Roundup (Dulce), Go-Gee-Ya (Dulce), Rio Grande White Water Race (Española), Pro-Rodeo Roundup (Farmington), Super Balloon Rally (Farmington), Connie Mack World Series Baseball Tournament (Farmington), Mid-Winter Rendezvous (Gallup), Rodeo at Grants (Grants), Region 9 National Soaring Contest (Hobbs), Corn and Turtle Races (Isleta), Southern New Mexico State Fair and Rodeo (Las Cruces), Overland Wind Sail Race (Lordsburg), Aspencade (Red River), Enchanted Circle Century Bike Tour (Red River), Great Milk Carton Boat Race (Roswell), Pecos Valley Horse Show (Roswell), Eastern New Mexico State Fair and Rodeo (Roswell), Aspenfest (Ruidoso), War Dances and Footraces

The Little Beaver Roundup in Dulce is just one of the events that reflects the Native American culture in the state.

New Mexico is one of the most popular states for hot air ballooning and the Albuquerque International Balloon Festival attracts pilots from around the world.

Southwest Ballet Company (Albuquerque), Albuquerque Opera Theater (Albuquerque), Gold Rush Days (Red River), Buffalo and Comanche dances (Santa Fe), Santa Fe Opera (Santa Fe), Spring Corn Dances (Santa Fe), Fiesta and Green Corn Dance (Santa Fe), Orchestra of Santa Fe (Santa Fe), Chamber Music Festival (Santa Fe), Sundown Dance (Taos), Taos Pueblo Deer or Matachina Dance (Taos), Taos Pueblo Dances (Taos), Chamber Music Festival (Taos).

Entertainment: Santa María Feast (Acoma Pueblo), San Juan Day (Acoma Pueblo), St. Peter's and St. Paul's Day (Acoma Pueblo), Santiago Day (Acoma Pueblo), St. Lawrence Day (Acoma Pueblo), Christmas Eve Luminarias (Acoma Pueblo), Space Hall of Fame Induction Ceremonies (Alamogordo), Old Town Fiesta (Albuquerque), San Pedro Day (Albuquerque), St. Ann's Day (Albuquerque), Pecos Feast (Albuquerque), Our Lady of Assumption Feast (Albuquerque), Spanish Fiesta and St. Augustine's Day (Albuquerque), New Mexico State Fair (Albuquerque), International Balloon Fiesta (Albuquerque), San Diego Feast Day (Albuquerque), Eddy County Fair (Artesia), Cimarron Days (Cimarron), Western

(Santa Fe), Santa Fe Rodeo (Sante Fe), Santa Fe Horse Show (Santa Fe), Conrad Hilton Open Golf Tournament (Socorro), Socorro County Fair and Rodeo (Socorro), Taos Rodeo (Taos).

Arts and Crafts: New Mexico Arts and Crafts Fair (Albuquerque), Fiesta Artística (Albuquerque), Butterfield Trail Days (Deming), Grants Arts and Crafts Fair (Grants), May Festival (Hobbs), Doña Ana Arts Council Renaissance Arts and Craftfaire (Las Cruces), Arts Festival (Ruidoso), Spanish Market (Santa Fe), Indian Market (Santa Fe), Invitational Antique Indian Art Show (Santa Fe), Folk Art Festival (Santa Fe), County Art Exhibit (Socorro), Taos Festival of Arts (Taos).

Music: Governor's Feast (Acoma Pueblo), St. Esteban Feast (Acoma Pueblo), Christmas Celebrations (Acoma Pueblo), New Year's Celebration (Albuquerque), King's Day (Albuquerque), Spring Corn Dances (Albuquerque), Dances (Albuquerque), Albuquerque Civic Light Opera (Albuquerque), New Mexico Symphony (Albuquerque),

Roundup (Cloudcroft), Curry County Fair (Clovis), Rockhound Roundup (Deming), Southwestern New Mexico State Fair (Deming), San Juan Feast Day (Española), Fiesta de Oñate (Española), Santa Clara Feast Day (Española), San Juan County Fair (Farmington), Cultural Heritage Festival (Farmington), Intertribal Indian Ceremonial (Gallup), Navajo Nation Fair (Gallup), Laguna Village Traditional Feast (Grants), San Juan Day (Grants), St. Peter's Day (Grants), Seama Village Feast (Grants), Mesita Village Feast (Grants), Encinal Village Feast (Grants), Fiesta (Grants), Paguate Village Feast (Grants), Paraje Village Feast (Grants), Cinco de Mayo Festival (Hobbs), Whole Enchilada Fiesta (Las Cruces), Our Lady of Guadalupe Fiesta (Las Cruces), Costumed Demonstrations (Las Vegas), Mescalero Apache Maidens' Ceremonial (Mescalero), Roosevelt County Heritage Days (Portales), Roosevelt County Fair (Portales), Peanut Valley Festival (Portales), Winter Carnival (Red River), Candelaria Day Celebration (Santa Fe), Riverman Day (Santa Fe), Fiesta at Cochiti Pueblo (Santa Fe), Fiesta at Santo Domingo Pueblo (Santa Fe), St. Lawrence Feast (Santa Fe), Santa Fe Fiesta (Santa Fe), Christmas Eve Celebrations (Santa Fe), Santa Rosa Day Celebration (Santa Rosa), Old Fort Days (Santa Rosa), Frontier Days (Silver City), Springfest (Socorro), San Geronimo Feast Day (Taos), Fiesta (Truth or Consequences), Sierra County Fair (Truth or Consequences), Hillsboro Apple Festival (Truth or Consequences), Piñata Festival (Tucumcari).

Tours: Trinity Site Tour (Alamogordo), Luminaria Tour (Albuquerque), Trek to Chimayo (Española), Ghost Town of Shakespeare (Lordsburg).

Theaters: New Mexico Repertory Theatre (Albuquerque), Albuquerque Little Theatre (Albuquerque), Flying X Chuckwagon (Carlsbad).

The Santa Fe Fiesta celebrates the color and culture of the historic city.

The Land and the Climate

New Mexico is bordered on the west by Arizona, on the north by Colorado, on the east by Oklahoma and Texas, and on the south by Texas and the Mexican states of Sonora and Chihuahua. The state has four main land regions: the Great Plains, the Rocky Mountains, the Basin and Range Region, and the Colorado Plateau.

The Great Plains cover the eastern one-third of New Mexico and are part of the vast plain that extends from Canada to Mexico. Many deep canyons have been cut by streams in the area to the west, where cattle and sheep are raised. Corn, wheat, peanuts, and cotton are grown here, and oil and natural gas are pumped from the ground.

The Rocky Mountains of New Mexico are in the north-central area and extend south almost to Santa Fe. In this region the Rio Grande (Great River) cuts between the main mountain ranges. East of the river is the Sangre de Cristo Range, which includes Wheeler Peak; at 13,160 feet above sea level, it is the highest point in the state. West of the river are the Nacimiento and Jemez Ranges. Oil, natural gas, and coal are found here, and some fruit and forest products are produced.

The Basin and Range Region extends south and west from the Rockies to the borders of Mexico and Arizona, covering about one-third of the state. This is an area of scattered mountain ranges, between which are basins—low places where streams have no outlet. Mines in the region produce gold, iron ore, copper, lead, zinc, and silver. There are numerous cattle ranches, and poultry, Angora goat, and sheep farms. Irrigation also allows fruits, vegetables, pecans, and cotton to be raised.

The Colorado Plateau is in northwestern New Mexico. This is a land of wide valleys and plains, deep canyons, sharp cliffs, and rugged mesas—flat-topped hills. To the south are badlands, made up of extinct volcanoes and arid lava plains. Uranium, coal, natural gas,

Chaco Canyon, in northwestern New Mexico, is a national monument preserving many ancient Indian dwellings.

The Rocky Mountains of New Mexico are a popular attraction for campers and climbers.

and oil are found here, and vegetables, and grains are the chief crops.

The most important river in New Mexico is the Rio Grande, which runs from north to south through the center of the state. Several large dams along the river form reservoirs for storage of irrigation water, which is essential to agriculture in most of the state. The Pecos, San Juan, Canadian, and Gila are other important New Mexican rivers whose waters are used for irrigation.

Dry air and warm temperatures are typical of New Mexico, where readings of 75 degrees Fahrenheit prevail in July. In winter, the north averages 35 degrees F. and the south, 55 degrees F. Only about 20 inches of rain and snow fall yearly, most of the snow in the northern mountains.

The History

People have lived in New Mexico for some 20,000 years. Ten-thousand-year-old projectile points and other artifacts discovered near Folsom, in northeastern New Mexico, indicate that Paleo-Indians hunted and lived in the region. From approximately 500 B.C. to A.D. 1200, the Mogollon people lived in the valleys along the New Mexico-Arizona border. These early farmers constructed circular huts, with earth and wood roofs covering storage pits, usually in the shadow of overhanging cliffs. Later they built rectangular above-ground multi-room houses. In northwestern New Mexico were the Anasazi, who developed a high form of civilization. They raised corn, beans, gourds, and cotton, and tamed wild turkeys, which were part of their diet. In the winter, the turkey feathers provided warm robes. The Anasazi and their descendants were cliff dwellers, who built many-storied apartment houses of adobe (sun-dried clay) using masonry techniques. One of them, at Chaco Canyon, extended over three acres and had more than 800 rooms. Before A.D. 1500, the nomadic Navaho settled near the Pueblo Indians and learned to raise corn and to weave cotton. The Navaho learned to raise sheep from the Spaniards, and wove the wool into spectacular rugs and blankets. From Mexicans they learned to make jewelry of silver and turquoise. The Apache and others used horses that had escaped from the Spaniards to pursue buffalo and lived in huts or tipis as they followed the herds and other game.

The Spaniards arrived in what is now New Mexico by accident. In 1528 an exploring party sent to seek gold in Florida was shipwrecked near the Texas coast. About 80 survivors, led by Álvar Núñez (known as Cabeza de Vaca), were captured by Indians and forced to work for them. Cabeza de Vaca and three shipmates finally escaped and made their way across Texas to the Rio Grande and thence to Mexico (New Spain). Their reports of rich Indian cities to the north led to further expeditions in search of these "Seven Cities of Cibola," which soon became legend.

In 1539 a Franciscan monk named Marcos de Niza set out to explore the territory, guided by one of the survivors of the shipwreck, an African slave named Estévan. De Niza arrived in what is now New Mexico in May of that year. From a nearby mesa, he viewed the Zuñi pueblo of Hawikuh, not far from present-day Gallup. But his guide was killed there, and he returned to Mexico after claiming the region for Spain.

De Niza's report so impressed the viceroy that in 1540 he sent Francisco Vásquez de Coronado and his army, with de Niza as guide, to explore what is now New Mexico and Arizona. The party searched for two years, but found no gold; The Indian pueblos did not have the wealth of the fabled Seven Cities. Coronado returned home in 1542 a disappointed man. In 1581 the region was explored by the monk Augustín Rodríguez and a soldier named Francisco Sánchez Chamuscado, who traveled up the Rio Grande from

Acoma, an Indian village about 50 miles west of Albuquerque, was established about 1100 A.D. This makes it the oldest continuously occupied site in the United States.

The monks who accompanied the Spanish explorers founded missions throughout the territory of New Spain.

Mexico. Their report, and that of the explorer Antonio de Espejo, persuaded the Spanish government to colonize New Mexico.

Don Juan de Oñate established the first Spanish settlement in New Mexico in 1598: the Pueblo of San Juan de Los Caballeros, near the Chama River. He was the first governor of the province. In 1610 his successor, Pedro de Peralta, moved the provincial capital to Santa Fe, which makes this city the oldest seat of government in the United States.

Roman Catholic missionaries set up schools to teach Christianity to the Indians, whom the civil authorities mistreated. As in Mexico, they were forced to do heavy labor and punished for worshipping their ancestral gods. By 1680 there were Spanish villages all along the Rio Grande. Then the Pueblo Indians, led by Popé, rebelled with Apache help and drove every colonist and missionary form New Mexico. More than 400 Spaniards were killed in the Pueblo Revolt.

But the Indians lacked a central government, and in 1692 Don Diego de Vargas, the Spanish governor, reconquered the province with little difficulty. For the next 125 years, Spanish colonists and Pueblo Indians co-existed uneasily.

New problems arose in the early 1800s, when American trappers and traders came into New Mexico. Spanish officials were determined to maintain control at any price, even that of forbidding trade with their nearest neighbors. They expelled the Americans, or put them into prison.

When Mexico threw off Spanish rule in 1821, New Mexico became part of the new empire to the south. William Becknell of Missouri brought the first wagons across the trackless plains and blazed what would become the Santa Fe Trail. As American settlers pushed farther west during the next 25 years, tensions grew between the United States and Mexico, resulting in the Mexican War of 1846. New Mexico became a United States Territory in 1850, two years after the war ended in an American victory. The original New Mexico Territory included what is now Arizona and part of present-day Colorado. The territory was enlarged on the south by the

Gadsden Purchase of 1853. The present boundaries of New Mexico were established in 1863, after Congress created the territories of Colorado and Arizona.

Confederate troops from Texas captured much of New Mexico, including Albuquerque and Santa Fe, early in the Civil War. But Union forces soon regained the region after two battles near Santa Fe—at Apache Canyon and Glorieta Pass. From 1862 to 1864, Colonel Kit Carson led the New Mexicans in a war that forced the Mescalero Apache and the Navaho onto reservations.

During the late 1870s, the Lincoln County War broke out when cattlemen and other factions vied for political control of the county. The murder of rancher John C. Tunstall touched off widespread violence in which "Billy the Kid" Bonney and other outlaws played a major part. In 1878 General Lewis "Lew" Wallace was appointed territorial governor and restored order by declaring martial law.

When the railroads arrived in the 1880s, New Mexico experienced rapid growth. The cattle industry flourished with access to distant markets, and settlers arrived from all parts of the country. Fear of the Apache Indians, who had long resisted American encroachment on their territory, diminished as most members of the tribe were confined to reservations. In 1885 the great Chiricahua Apache chief Geronimo (Goyathlay) fled from an Arizona reservation with some of his warriors and terrified settlers with raids from his base in Mexico. But when Geronimo and his band surrendered to General Nelson A. Miles in 1886, the Apache Wars were over.

In 1912 New Mexico became the 47th state, with a population of some 330,000. The mining of copper, silver, and other mineral resources had become a thriving industry, although farming and ranching remained important. In 1916 the Mexican revolutionary Francisco "Pancho" Villa and his men raided Columbus, New Mexico, and killed 17 Americans. General John J. Pershing crossed the Mexican border, but failed to find Villa in the northern mountains. A year later, the United States entered World War I, and more than 17,000 New Mexicans served in the armed forces.

One of the legendary outlaws of New Mexico was William H. Bonney, better known as Billy the Kid (1859–1881).

The narrow gauge railroads equipped with steam engines brought settlers to New Mexico. They are now a popular tourist attraction.

A prolonged drought in the 1920s hurt the farming and ranching industries of New Mexico a decade before the nation suffered through the Great Depression of the 1930s. When livestock prices dropped, many banks closed and ranchers were forced into bankruptcy. The economy revived with the discovery of oil and the mining of huge potash deposits in the Carlsbad area.

In 1941 a New Mexico regiment, the 200th Coast Artillery, was stationed in the Philippines when the Japanese attacked Pearl Harbor and the United States entered World War II. The 200th and other American forces were overwhelmed by Japanese troops on the Bataan Peninsula, and those who were not killed spent more than three years in Japanese prison camps under intolerable conditions. During the war, the U.S. government established the town and laboratory of Los Alamos to develop the atomic bomb, which was first exploded in a test near Alamogordo on July 16, 1945. Within weeks the bomb was dropped on the Japanese cities of Hiroshima and Nagasaki, with devastating results. Survivors are still being treated for the effects of radiation more than 40 years after the surrender of Japan.

In the postwar period, New Mexico has enlarged its role as a scientific research center, especially in the field of atomic power. Rocket and missile research has been conducted at White Sands since 1945, and uranium, a component in nuclear fuels and weapons, was discovered in the state in 1950. Tourism has grown rapidly since the vast caverns at Carlsbad became a national park in 1930. Santa Fe and Taos are vital centers for the arts and attract many visitors. Industries like oil and uranium now yield more than $6 billion per year.

Between 1940 and 1960 the population of New Mexico doubled, due to the expansion of the scientific and space industries that settled in the region. This growth and expansion continued into the 1970s, but at a decreased rate. In the late 1960s and early 1970s many struggles erupted between Native Americans and Anglo-Americans over ownership of the land.

The completion of the San Juan-Chama water project in the 1970s brought water to north-central New Mexico through tunnels from branches of the San Juan River to the Rocky Mountain area. The construction and improvement of tourist and winter sports facilities have increased state income and made New Mexico a popular vacation destination.

Indian dances and ceremonies are still performed near the *pueblos* (indian villages) of New Mexico.

Education

Education in New Mexico goes back to the early 1600s, when Spanish missionaries started schools for the Indians. Archbishop Jean Baptiste Lamy founded the region's first permanent school, in Santa Fe, in 1853. The first library had opened there two years earlier. St. Michael's College, established in 1859, was New Mexico's first institution of higher education, and five others were founded before the turn of the century: New Mexico State University (1888), the University of New Mexico (1889), New Mexico Institute of Mining and Technology (1889), New Mexico Highlands University (1893), and Western New Mexico University (1893).

One of the nation's most innovative and well-known undergraduate institutions, Saint Johns College, is located in Santa Fe, with a sister campus in Annapolis, Maryland.

Artist Georgia O'Keeffe (1887–1986) lived in the artists' colony in Taos, and painted numerous landscapes of the stark New Mexico desert.

The People

About 48 percent of the people of New Mexico live in metropolitan areas such as Albuquerque, Roswell, and Santa Fe. Most New Mexicans are descendants of the Indians and of the Spanish- and English-speaking people who settled the area. About 94 percent of them were born in the United States. The majority of New Mexicans are Protestants, including Baptists, Episcopalians, Methodists, and Presbyterians. Roman Catholics make up the state's largest single religious community.

Famous People
Many famous people were born in the state of New Mexico. Here are a few:

Bruce Cabot 1904-72, Carlsbad. Film actor: *King Kong, Cat Ballou*

Jan Clayton 1917-83, Tularosa. Television actress: *Lassie*

John Denver b. 1943, Roswell. Pop singer

Pete Domenici b. 1932, Albuquerque. Congressional leader

Conrad Hilton 1887-1979, San Antonio. Hotelier

Dolores Huerta b. 1930, Dawson. Union leader

Ralph Kiner b. 1922, Santa Rita. Hall of Fame baseball player

Harrison Schmitt b. 1935, Santa Rita. Astronaut

Kim Stanley b. 1925, Tularosa. Stage and film actress: *Bus Stop, The Goddess*

Slim Summerville 1892-1946, Albuquerque. Film actor: *All Quiet on the Western Front, The Hoodlum Saint*

Al Unser b. 1939, Albuquerque. Champion auto racer

Bobby Unser b. 1934, Albuquerque. Champion auto racer

Pete Domenici is a Republican senator who has represented New Mexico in Congress since 1973.

Colleges and Universities
There are many colleges and universities in New Mexico. Here are the more prominent, with their locations, dates of founding, and enrollments.

Eastern New Mexico University, Portales, 1934, 3,360

New Mexico Highlands University, Las Vegas, 1893, 2,142

New Mexico Institute of Mining and Technology, Socorro, 1889, 1,264

New Mexico State University, Las Cruces, 1888, 12,957

St. Johns College, Santa Fe, 1964, 450

University of New Mexico, Albuquerque, 1889, 19,937

Western New Mexico University, Silver City, 1893, 2,050

Where To Get More Information
New Mexico Department of Tourism
P.O. Box 20003
Santa Fe, NM 87503
or call, 1-800-545-2040

Texas

The state seal of Texas, adopted in 1839, is circular. In the center is a star of five points encircled by olive and live oak branches. The live oak branch represents strength, and the olive branch stands for peace. Around the seal is printed "The State of Texas."

TEXAS
At a Glance

Capital: Austin

Major Industries: Machinery, transportation equipment, petroleum, livestock

Major Crops: Cotton, grain, fruits, nuts

State Bird: Mockingbird

State Flower: Bluebonnet

Size: 266,807 square miles (2nd largest)
Population: 17,655,650 (3rd largest)

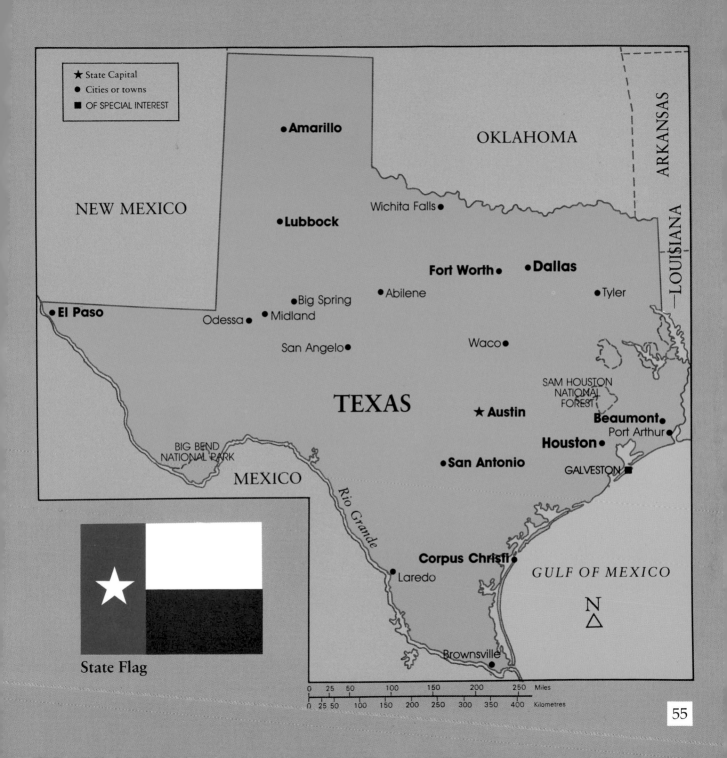

State Capital
Cities or towns
OF SPECIAL INTEREST

OKLAHOMA

ARKANSAS

NEW MEXICO

●Amarillo

Wichita Falls●

LOUISIANA

●Lubbock

Fort Worth ●Dallas

●Big Spring ●Abilene ●Tyler

●El Paso Odessa● ●Midland

San Angelo● Waco●

TEXAS

SAM HOUSTON
NATIONAL
FOREST

★ Austin

Beaumont●
Port Arthur●

BIG BEND
NATIONAL PARK Houston●

MEXICO ●San Antonio

GALVESTON■

Rio Grande

Corpus Christi●

GULF OF MEXICO

N
△

Laredo●

Brownsville●

0 25 50 100 150 200 250 Miles

0 25 50 100 150 200 250 300 350 400 Kilometres

State Flag

55

State Flag

The state flag of Texas was adopted in 1876. On the staff end is a broad blue vertical stripe, and the rest of the flag has a broad white stripe over a broad red stripe. In the center of the blue stripe is a white star, representing the Lone Star State. The blue bar stands for loyalty, the white bar for purity, and the red bar for bravery.

State Salute to the Flag

The salute to the Texas flag is: "Honor the Texas Flag; I pledge allegiance to thee, Texas, one and indivisible."

State Motto

Friendship
The motto was adopted in 1930.

El Camino del Rio, Spanish for "The River Road," is a scenic drive through mountainous terrain.

State Capital

Austin was chosen capital of Texas in 1839, six years before it became a state.

State Name and Nicknames

In 1690, the Spanish named their first mission in the area "St. Francis de los Tejas," taking the word from the Caddo Indian language. *Tejas,* or *teysha,* meant "hello, friend."

The most common nickname for Texas is the *Lone Star State.* Both the state seal and state flag bear a single star, representing the fact that Texas was once an independent republic. The state is also called the *Beef State* for its cattle production and the *Banner State* because of its leading position in many fields.

State Flower

The bluebonnet, *Lupinus subcarnosis,* was named the state flower in 1901.

State Tree

In 1919, Texas adopted the pecan, *Carya illinoensis,* as state tree.

State Bird

The mockingbird, *Mimus polyglottos,* was selected state bird in 1927.

State Stone

Petrified palmwood was adopted as the state stone in 1969.

State Shell

In 1987, the state legislature selected the lightning whelk as state shell.

State Dish

The Texas legislature adopted chili as state dish in 1977.

State Gem

Texas blue topaz was chosen state gem in 1969.

State Fish

In 1989, Guadalupe bass was adopted as state fish.

State Plays

Texas adopted four state plays in 1979. They are: *The Lone Star, Texas, Beyond the Sundown,* and *Fandangle.*

State Songs

In 1928, "Texas, Our Texas," by William J. Marsh and Gladys Yoakum Wright, was named the state song. "Bluebonnets," with words by Julia D. Booth and music by Lora C. Crockett, was selected as the state flower song in 1933.

Population

The population of Texas in 1992 was 17,655,650, making it the third most populous state. There are 63.24 people per square mile.

Industries

The principal industries of the state of Texas are trade, services, and manufacturing. The chief manufactured products are machinery, transportation equipment, foods, refined petroleum, and apparel.

Agriculture

The chief crops of the state are cotton, grain sorghum, grains, vegetables, citrus and other fruits, pecans, and peanuts. Texas is also a livestock state; there are estimated to be some 13.4 million cattle, 500,000 hogs and pigs, 2 million sheep, and 17.2 million chickens and turkeys on its farms. Pine and cypress trees are harvested. Cement, stone, sand, and gravel are important mineral resources. Commercial fishing brings in some $170.1 million each year.

Government

The governor of Texas is elected to a four-year term, as are the lieutenant governor, attorney general, commissioner of agriculture, commissioner of the general land office, comptroller, and treasurer. The state legislature consists of a 31-member senate and a 150-member house of representatives. The senators, who serve four year terms, are elected from 31 senatorial districts. Representatives, who serve two-year terms, are elected from 150 representative districts. The most recent state constitution was adopted in 1876. In addition to its two U.S. senators, Texas has 30 representatives in the U.S. House of Representatives. The state has 32 votes in the electoral college.

Sports

Texas is sports-mad. The Little League World Series was won by Houston teams in 1950 and 1966. On the collegiate level, Texas

The Lyndon B. Johnson Space Center in Houston is the headquarters of America's manned space program.

Western University won the NCAA basketball championship in 1966, while the University of Texas won the National Invitation Tournament in 1978. In football, the Orange Bowl has been won by the University of Texas (1949, 1965), and Rice (1947); the Sugar Bowl has been won by Texas Christian University (1936, 1939), Texas A & M (1940), the University of Texas (1948), and Baylor (1957); and the Cotton Bowl has been won by Texas Christian (1937, 1957), Rice (1938, 1950,

The Astrodome, the world's first indoor stadium, is the home of the Houston Astros and Houston Oilers.

1954), Texas A & M (1941, 1968, 1986, 1988), the University of Texas (1943, 1946, 1953, 1962, 1964, 1969, 1970, 1973, 1982), Southern Methodist University (1949, 1983), and the University of Houston (1977, 1980). The University of Texas has also won the NCAA baseball championship (1949, 1950, 1975, 1983).

On the professional level, the Dallas Cowboys of the National Football League play in Texas Stadium, the Texas Rangers of the American League play baseball in Arlington Stadium, and the Dallas Mavericks of the National Basketball Association play in Reunion Arena. The Houston Astros of the National League play baseball in the Astrodome, which they share with the Houston Oilers of the National Football League. The Houston Rockets of the National Basketball Association play in the Summit, while the San Antonio Spurs play in the HemisFair Arena.

Major Cities

Austin (population 465,622). Founded in 1839, the capital city was named after Stephen F. Austin. This city of handsome buildings and beautiful homes is also a science, research, education, and government center.

Things to see in Austin: State Capitol, Old Land Office (1857), Texas Confederate Museum, Daughters of the Republic of Texas Museum, Governor's Mansion (1856), Texas Memorial Museum, Archer M. Huntington Art Gallery in the Ransom Center, Archer M. Huntington Art Gallery in the Art Building, Lyndon Baines Johnson Library and Museum, Harry Ransom Center, Laguna Gloria Art Museum, Elisabet Ney Museum, O. Henry Home and Museum, French Legation Museum (1841), McKinney Falls State Park, Neill-Cochran House (1855), and Austin Area Garden Center.

The Lyndon B. Johnson Library and Museum in Austin houses exhibits on Johnson and the presidency.

Dallas, the second-largest city in Texas behind Houston, is a thriving business center for the Southwest.

Dallas (population 1,007,618). Founded in 1841, Dallas was as a trading post for the Caddo Indians. Today it is a trade, manufacturing, and transportation center.

Things to see in Dallas:
Age of Steam Railroad Museum, the Hall of State, Dallas Museum of Natural History, Dallas Aquarium, Science Place, Dallas Civic Garden Center, Telephone Pioneer Museum of Texas, Dallas Museum of Art, Dallas Market Center Complex, Old City Park, Biblical Arts Center, Dallas Zoo, John F. Kennedy Memorial Plaza, Kennedy Historical Exhibit, and White Rock Lake Park.

El Paso (population 515,342). Founded in 1827, El Paso had been the site of several missions since 1659. It was completely Mexican until it was captured by U.S. forces in 1846, during the Mexican War. Today, El Paso is a manufacturing, military, and education center.

Things to see in El Paso:
Fort Bliss, El Paso Museum of Art, Chamizal National Memorial, Magoffin Home State Historic Site, Wilderness Park Museum, U.S. Army Air Defense Artillery Museum, El Paso Museum of History, and Del Camino Bullfight Museum.

Houston (population 1,630,864). Founded in 1836, the town was named for Sam Houston and was the first capital of the Republic of Texas. Today, Houston is a manufacturing giant, as well as being an aerospace headquarters and the nation's third busiest port.

Things to see in Houston:
Houston Civic Center, Museum of Fine Arts, Contemporary Arts Museum, Bayou Bend Collection, Houston Zoological Gardens, Museum of Natural Science, Burke Baker Planetarium, Armand Bayou Nature Center, Houston Arboretum and Nature Center, Rothko Chapel, NASA Lyndon B.

Johnson Space Center, Astrodome, AstroWorld, WaterWorld, Port of Houston, San Jacinto Battleground, Battleship Texas, Allen's Landing Park, and Old Market Square.

San Antonio (population 935,933). Founded in 1718, San Antonio was originally The Mission San Antonio de Valero (the Alamo). Over its long history it has been under six flags: France, Spain, Mexico, the Republic of Texas, the Confederate States of America, and the United States of America. Today, this beautiful old city is a modern, prosperous community that retains much of the flavor of its past.

Things to see in San Antonio: The Alamo (1718), Menger Hotel, HemisFair Plaza, La Villita, Cos House, Hertzberg Circus Collection, Paseo del Rio, San Fernando Cathedral, Military Plaza, Spanish Governor's Palace (1749), José Antonio Navarro State Historic Site, Market Square, Mission Nuestra Señora de La

The Tigua Reservation in El Paso offers visitors a look at Native American culture through dances and arts and crafts.

Purisima Concepción de Acuna (1731), Mission San José y San Miguel de Aguayo (1720), Espada Dam, Mission San Juan Capistrano (1731), Mission San Francisco de la Espada (1731), Espada Aqueduct (1735), Vietnam Veterans Memorial, Institute of Texan Cultures, Tower of the Americas, Marion Koogler McNay Art Museum, San Antonio Museum of Art, Southwest Craft Center, Plaza Theater of Wax,

Buckhorn Hall of Horns and Hall of Texas History, Steves Homestead (1876), Yturri-Edmunds Home and Mill (1840-60), Witte Museum, Texas Ranger Museum-Memorial Hall, Zoological Gardens and Aquarium, Japanese Tea Gardens, Brackenridge *Eagle*, San Antonio Botanical Gardens, Fort Sam Houston Museum and Landmark, Water Park USA, Natural Bridge Caverns, and Cascade Caverns Park.

Places to Visit

The National Park Service maintains 15 areas in the state of Texas: Big Bend National Park, Guadalupe Mountains National Park, Padre Island National Seashore, Lyndon B. Johnson National Historical Park, San Antonio Missions National Historical Park, Fort Davis National Historic Site, Amistad National Recreation Area, Lake Meredith National Recreation Area,

Alibates Flint Quarries National Monument, Chamizal National Memorial, Big Thicket National Preserve, Angelina National Forest, Davy Crockett National Forest, Sabine National Forest, and Sam Houston National Forest. In addition, there are 55 state recreation areas.

Abilene: Buffalo Gap Historic Village. Visitors may tour restored buildings, including

a courthouse and jail.

Angleton: Varner-Hogg Plantation State Historical Park. This stately home was built around 1835.

Arlington: Six Flags Over Texas. This amusement park has over 100 rides.

Baytown: Anahuac National Wildlife Refuge. Migrating and wintering waterfowl can be seen on this 24,293-acre tract.

Beaumont: John J. French Museum. Built in 1845, this is a restored Greek revival house.

Bonham: Fort Inglish. This settlement contains a replica of the 1837 blockhouse built to protect settlers from the Indians.

Brackettville: Alamo Village Movie Location. Gunfights and entertainment are featured on this compound containing the set for the film *The Alamo.*

Brenham: Mrs. Sam Houston House. Built around 1835, Houston's widow bought this house in 1863.

Burnet: Fort Croghan Museum. This was one of the frontier forts built from 1848-49.

Comanche: Old Cora. Built in 1856, this is the oldest existing courthouse in the state.

Corsicana: Pioneer Village. The village contains many

The Buffalo Gap Historic Village is a restored frontier settlement that brings the past back to visitors.

restored buildings, including a blacksmith shop and gristmill.

Del Rio: Judge Roy Bean Visitor Center. This saloon-courtroom served the man who was the "Law West of the Pecos."

Denison: Eisenhower Birthplace State Historic Site. This restored house is where the late president was born.

Fairfield: Burlington-Rock Island Railroad Museum. Railroad materials are stored in a 1906 depot.

Fort Stockton: Annie Riggs Hotel Museum. Built in 1899, this turn-of-the-century hotel features displays on local history.

Fort Worth: Amon Carter Museum. One of the finest collections of American art is housed in this museum.

Fredericksburg: Pioneer Museum. Several buildings contain relics of early German settlers.

Galveston: *Elissa,* "The Tall Ship for Texas," Pier 21. This sailing ship was launched in 1877.

Goliad: Presidio La Bahia. Built in 1749, this was the most fought-over fort in Texas history.

Granbury: Granbury Opera House. Built in 1886, this

Alamo Village in Brackettville is a family attraction built around the movie set used for John Wayne's The Alamo, *filmed in 1959.*

restored theater is in the historic town square.

Hereford: National Cowgirl Hall of Fame and Western Heritage Center. Exhibits about notable women in rodeo history are featured.

Jefferson: Freeman Plantation. Built in 1850, this restored house is furnished with antiques.

Johnson City: Lyndon B.

Johnson Boyhood Home. Built in 1901, this home housed the Johnson family from 1913 to 1934.

Kerrville: Y.O. Ranch. This working ranch, dating back to 1880, also features African wildlife.

Mason: Fort Mason. This fort was Robert E. Lee's last command before the Civil War.

McKinney: Bolin Wildlife Museum. More than 100 animals are exhibited.

Nacogdoches: Sterne-Hoya Home. This pioneer house was built in 1830.

Paris: Sam Bell Maxey House State Historical Structure. Built in 1867, this was the home of a Confederate general and U.S. senator.

Port Arthur: Pompeiian Villa. Built in 1900, this is a replica of a Pompeiian home of A.D. 79.

Port Isabel: Port Isabel Lighthouse State Historic Structure. The lighthouse, built in 1851, is the site of the last land battle of the Civil War.

San Angelo: Fort Concho National Historic Landmark. The fort contains 21 restored buildings.

San Marcos: Wonder World. This is a cave created by an earthquake.

Shamrock: Pioneer West Museum. Pioneer artifacts are housed in a renovated hotel.

Stephenville: Historical House Museum Complex. An English cottage (1869) and church (1899) are among the buildings featured here.

Temple: Railroad and Pioneer Museum. Exhibits are displayed in an 1881 Santa Fe depot.

Texarkana: Perot Theater. Built in 1924, this is a performing arts facility.

Tyler: Tyler Rose Garden. More than 30,000 plants of 400 different varieties are displayed on 15 acres.

Uvalde: Grand Opera House. This historic theater was built in 1891.

Waco: Texas Ranger Hall of Fame and Museum. Exhibits depict the 150-year history of the Texas Rangers.

Wichita Falls: Kell House. This home, built in 1909, contains the original family furnishings.

Wimberley: Pioneer Town. This reproduction of an 1880 town features entertainment from June through August.

Woodville: Heritage Garden Village. Many restored buildings represent 19th-century life in Texas.

Events

There are many events and organizations that schedule activities of various kinds in the state of Texas. Here are some of them.

Sports: Hardin-Simmons University Rodeo (Abilene), West Texas Fair and Rodeo (Abilene), Southwest PGA Golf Classic (Abilene), Lone Star Circuit Finals Rodeo (Abilene), Big Bend Bash (Alpine), Boys Ranch Rodeo (Amarillo), National Old Timers Rodeo (Amarillo), Livestock Show (Austin), Legends of Golf (Austin), Cowboy Capital PRCA Rodeo (Bandera), Sandcastle and Sand Sculpture Contest (Brazosport), Bass Tournament (Brownwood), Childress County Old Settlers' Reunion (Childress), Sheriff's Posse PRCA Rodeo (Cleburne), XIT Rodeo and Reunion (Dalhart), Cotton Bowl Football Game (Dallas), Virginia Slims Tennis Tournament (Dallas), Byron Nelson Golf Classic (Dallas), PRCA Rodeo (Del Rio), Superbull (Del Rio), Amistad Navy Regatta (Del Rio), Jim Bob Altizer International Roping Events (Del Rio), North Texas State Fair and Rodeo (Denton), Edinburg 10K Run (Edinburg), Southwestern International Livestock Show and Rodeo (El Paso), Coors World Championship Rodeo Finals (El Paso), John Hancock Sun Bowl Football Classic (El Paso), IPRA Rodeo (Fort Stockton), Sul Ross State University NIRA Rodeo (Fort Stockton), Goliad County Fair and Rodeo (Goliad), Houston Livestock Show Parade and Rodeo (Houston), PRCA Lion's Club Championship Rodeo (Jasper), Texas A & I National Intercollegiate Rodeo (Kingsville), Mesquite Championship Rodeo (Mesquite), Palo Pinto County Livestock Association Rodeo (Mineral Wells), Torneo de Amistad (Mission), Mount Pleasant TRA and CRA Championship Rodeo (Mount Pleasant), Sand Hills Hereford and Quarter Horse Show and Rodeo (Odessa), Top O'Texas Rodeo. RCA (Pampa), CRA Annual Rodeo (Paris), "West of the Pecos" Rodeo (Pecos), Deep-Sea Roundup (Port Aransas), Fishing Rodeo (Port Arthur), Texas International Fishing Tournament (Port Isabel), Livestock Exposition and Rodeo (San Antonio), Texas Water Safari (San Marcos), Republic of Texas Chilympiad (San Marcos), Texas State High School Rodeo Finals (Seguin), Western Texas College Rodeo (Snyder),

American Junior Rodeo Finals (Snyder), Goat Cook-off and Goat Roping (Sonora), Hopkins County Stew Contest and Star Night (Sulphur Springs), CRA Finals Rodeo (Sulphur Springs), Junior Indoor Rodeo (Sweetwater), Belton PRCA Rodeo and July 4th Celebration (Temple), Four States Fair and Rodeo (Texarkana), Rose Bowl Chile Cook-off (Tyler), Air Fiesta (Uvalde), Cactus Jack Festival and Horse Races (Uvalde), Big Country Marathon (Van Horn), Santa Rosa Roundup (Vernon), PRCA Rodeo (Victoria), Great Texas Raft Race (Waco), Heart O'Texas Fair and Rodeo (Waco), Heart O'Texas Speedway (Waco), Texas Ranch Roundup (Wichita Falls), Hotter 'n Hell Bicycle Ride (Wichita Falls), Red River Chili Championship (Wichita Falls).

Arts and Crafts: Buffalo Gap Fine Arts Festival (Abilene), Highland Lakes Bluebonnet Trail (Austin), Old Pecan Street Arts Festival (Austin), Laguna Gloria Fiesta (Austin), Highland Lakes Arts and Crafts Trail (Austin), Kaleidoscope (Beaumont), Beaumont Heritage Society Antique Show (Beaumont), Gem and Mineral Show (Big Spring), Bois d'Arc Festival (Bonham), Pecan Valley Art Festival (Brownwood), Gem and Mineral Show (Fredericksburg), Arts and Crafts Festival (Fritch), Williamson County Gem and Mineral Show (Georgetown), Bond's Alley Arts Festival (Hillsboro), Texas State Arts and Crafts Fair (Kerrville), Borderfest (Laredo), Spring Arts Festival (Longview), Lubbock Arts Festival (Lubbock), American Poinsettia Society Annual Flower Show (Mission), High Plains Gem and Mineral Show (Plainview), Spring Fling Festival (Wichita Falls).

Music: Greater Southwest Music Festival (Amarillo), Amarillo Symphony (Amarillo), Texas Fiddlers' Contest and Reunion (Athens), Austin Symphony (Austin), Square Dance Festival (Big Spring), Jazz Festival (Bryan), Corpus Christi Symphony (Corpus Christi), Texas Jazz Festival (Corpus Christi), Summer Bayfront Concerts (Corpus Christi), World's Champion Fiddlers' Festival (Crockett), Bluegrass Festival (Crockett), Dallas Ballet (Dallas), Dallas Opera (Dallas), Lyric Opera of Dallas (Dallas), Dallas Symphony (Dallas), Denton Jazz Fest (Denton), El Paso Symphony Orchestra (El

The top cowboys are bucked to fame at the XIT Rodeo in Dalhart. In the 1880s, the XIT Ranch spread for three million acres.

Paso), National Polka Festival (Ennis), Fort Worth Symphony (Fort Worth), Fort Worth Opera (Fort Worth), Fiddle Festival and Flea Market (Groesbeck), Rio Grande Music Festival (Harlingen), Houston International Festival (Houston), Summer concerts (Houston), Houston Ballet (Houston), Houston Grand Opera (Houston), Houston Symphony (Houston), Texas Opera Theater (Houston), Kerrville Folk Festival (Kerrville), Kerrville Bluegrass Festival (Kerrville), Lubbock Symphony (Lubbock), International Rio Grande Valley Music Festival (McAllen), Midland-Odessa Symphony (Midland), Band Concerts (Paris), Pleasure Island Music Festival (Port Arthur), Great Country River Festival (San Antonio), San Antonio Symphony (San Antonio), Sahawe Indian Dance Ceremonials (Uvalde), Bach Festival (Victoria), Falls Fest (Wichita Falls), Jones Country Music Park (Woodville).

Entertainment: Abilene Junior Livestock Show (Abilene), Fiesta Bandana (Abilene), Jim Wells County Fair (Alice), Tri-State Fair (Amarillo), Cowboy Morning Breakfast (Amarillo), Brazoria County Fair (Angleton), Shrimporee (Aransas Pass), Black-Eyed Pea Jamboree

(Athens), Austin Aqua Festival (Austin), Bandera County Fair (Bandera), Hunter's Barbecue (Bandera), Neches River Festival (Beaumont), South Texas State Fair (Beaumont), Rattlesnake Roundup (Big Spring), Old Settlers Reunion (Big Spring), Howard County Fair (Big Spring), Fannin County Free Fair (Bonham), Frontier Fair (Brackettville), Fort Clark Cavalry Days (Brackettville), Blessing of the Fishing Fleet (Brazosport), Great Mosquito Festival (Brazosport), Shrimp Boil and Auction (Brazosport), Texas Independence Day Celebration (Brenham), Maifest (Brenham), Washington County Fair (Brenham), Charro Days (Brownsville), Rattlesnake Roundup (Brownwood), Bluebonnet Festival (Burnet), Comanche County Powwow (Comanche), Texas Renaissance Festival (Conroe), Buccaneer Days (Corpus Christi), Bayfest (Corpus Christi), Harbor Lights Celebration (Corpus Christi), Derrick Days (Corsicana), Cotton Bowl Festival (Dallas), Boat Show (Dallas), Scarborough Faire Renaissance Festival (Dallas), State Fair of Texas (Dallas), Nights in Old San Felipe Del Rio (Del Rio), Fiesta de Amistad (Del Rio), Western Days (Denison), 4-H Youth Fair and Auction (Denton), Texas

Wildflower Day (Denton), Victorian Christmas (Denton), April Fest (Eagle Lake), Fiesta Hidalgo (Edinburg), Pan American Days (Edinburg), Bronco Days (Edinburg), El Paso Street Festival (El Paso), Fiesta de las Flores (El Paso), Border Folk Festival (El Paso), Sun Carnival (El Paso), Fiesta de San Juan (Fort Stockton), Southwestern Exposition, Fat Stock Show (Fort Worth), Chisholm Trail Roundup (Fort Worth), Night in Old Fredericksburg (Fredericksburg), Gillespie County Fair (Fredericksburg), Kristkindl Market (Fredericksburg), World's Largest Fish Fry (Fritch), Mardi Gras (Galveston), Galveston Island Shrimp Festival (Galveston), Cinco de Mayo Fiesta (Goliad), Come and Take It Celebration (Gonzales), Hunt County Fair (Greenville), Red Stocking Follies (Groesbeck), Cotton Week (Harlingen), Confederate Air Force Air Show (Harlingen), Hill County Fair (Hillsboro), Bond's Alley Holiday Bazaar (Hillsboro), Houston Anniversary Celebration (Houston), Texas Renaissance Festival (Houston), Christmas Boat Lane (Houston), World of Christmas (Houston), Greek Festival (Houston), Western Week (Jacksonville), Tomato Fest (Jacksonville),

Longhorn Trail Drive (Kerrville), Kerr County Fair (Kerrville), Kleberg/Kenedy Counties Junior Livestock Show and Fair (Kingsville), Heritage Roundup (Kingsville), Fiesta de Colores (Kingsville), Fayette County Country Fair (La Grange), George Washington's Birthday Celebration (Laredo), Laredo International Fair and Exposition (Laredo), Frontier Days (Laredo), "Fiestas Patrias" (Laredo), Southwest Junior Livestock Show (Lubbock), Panhandle South Plains Fair (Lubbock), Highland Hereford Show and Bull Sale (Marfa), Marfa Lights Festival (Marfa), Central East Texas Fair (Marshall), Wonderland of Lights (Marshall), Candlelight Posada (McAllen), Texas Citrus Fiesta (Mission), Titus County Fair (Mount Pleasant), Children's May Festival and Masquerade (New Braunfels), Comal County Fair (New Braunfels), Wurstfest (New Braunfels), Cultural Carnival (Odessa), Anderson County Fair (Palestine), Top O'Texas Junior Livestock Show and Sale (Pampa), Red River Valley Exposition (Paris), Pioneer Roundup (Plainview), Lighting of the Boats (Port Aransas), Cajun Festival (Port Arthur), Mexican Independence Day Festival (Port Arthur), Cayman Island Weekend (Port Arthur), CavOILcade (Port Arthur), Calhoun County Fair (Port Lavaca), OysterFest (Rockport), Sea Fair Festival (Rockport), Gathering of the Clans (Salado), Frontier Days (San Angelo), Fiestas Patrias (San Angelo), Christmas at Old Fort Concho (San Angelo), Texas Independence Day and Flag Celebration (San Antonio), Alamo Memorial Service (San Antonio), Fiesta San Antonio (San Antonio), San Antonio Festival (San Antonio), Boerne Berges Fest (San Antonio), Texas Folklife Festival (San Antonio), Youth Livestock Show (Seguin), Guadalupe County Fair (Seguin), Guadalupe County Pecan Festival (Seguin), St. Patrick's Day Celebration (Shamrock), Texoma Livestock Exposition (Sherman), Scurry County Fair (Snyder), White Buffalo Days (Snyder), Game Dinner (Sonora), Spring Break (South Padre Island), Christmas Boat Parade of Lights (South Padre Island), Folklife Festival (Sulphur Springs), Hopkins County Dairy Festival (Sulphur Springs), Rattlesnake Roundup (Sweetwater), Mainland Springfest (Texas City), Shrimp Boil (Texas City), Fair on the Square (Texas City), East Texas Fair (Tyler), Texas Rose Festival (Tyler), Livestock Show (Van Horn), Culberson County Fair (Van Horn), Victoria Jaycees Stockshow (Victoria), Confederate Air Force Show (Victoria), Texas Zoo Fest (Victoria), Texas Air Expo (Waco), Christmas on the Brazos (Waco), Sugarfest (Weslaco), Noche en Weslaco (Weslaco), Viva Weslaco (Weslaco), Texas Weapon Collectors Association Gun and Knife Shows (Wichita Falls), Fantasy of Lights (Wichita Falls), Tyler County Fair (Woodville).

Tours: Candlelight Tours (Houston), Houston Azalea Trail (Houston), Pilgrimage to the Alamo (San Antonio), Fiesta de las Luminarias (San Antonio).

Theater: Zilker Park Hillside Theater (Austin), *Texas* (Canyon), Summer musicals (Dallas), Southwest Repertory Organization (El Paso), Shakespeare in the Park (Fort Worth), Casa Mañana Musicals (Fort Worth), Easter Fires Pageant (Fredericksburg), Dickens on the Strand (Galveston), *The Lone Star* Outdoor Drama (Galveston), Theatre Under the Stars (Houston), Smith/Ritch Point Theatre (Kerrville), Summer Mummers (Midland), Pickwick Players (Midland), Shakespeare Festival (Odessa), Permian Playhouse (Odessa), Frances Ann Lutcher Theater (Orange), Summer Festival (San Antonio).

The Land and the Climate

Texas is bordered on the west by New Mexico and the Mexican state of Chihuahua, on the north by Oklahoma and Arkansas, on the east by Arkansas and Louisiana, and on the south by the Gulf of Mexico and the Mexican states of Tamaulipas, Nuevo Leon, and Coahuila. Texas has four main land regions: the West Gulf Coastal Plain, the North-Central Plains, the Great Plains, and the Basin and Range Region.

The West Gulf Coastal Plain is a strip of land from 150 to 300 miles wide along the Gulf Coast; it is part of a larger area that stretches from Texas to Florida. The shorelands of the warm Gulf of Mexico include subtropical regions and fertile areas that specialize in winter vegetables and fruits. Commercial fishermen ply the waters of the Gulf for shrimp, sea trout, and red snapper. Timber and wood products are important industries, and cattle are pastured on huge ranches. Large deposits of coal, natural gas, oil, salt, and sulfur are also found in the region.

The North-Central Plains, which form a huge thumb-shaped area in the north-central part of the state, have the largest population and some of the best farmland in Texas. Thick grasses make this an ideal region for cattle raising. Cotton, grains, fruit, and pecans are grown, and numerous wells produce oil and natural gas.

The Great Plains extend south from the western half of the Panhandle to the lower part of the state. The altitude here ranges from about 700 feet above sea level to more than 4,000 feet in the west. The region has vast wheat farms and the richest petroleum and natural gas fields in the country. Building stone and salt are quarried here, and there are many cattle, goat, and sheep ranches.

The Basin and Range Region is also called the Trans-Pecos. It is the southern extension of the Rocky Mountains: a land of high, dry plains in the far western part of the state. Livestock and pecans are among the region's agricultural products.

Davis Mountain State Park in west Texas is a popular place for hiking and nature study.

Corpus Christi, on the Gulf of Mexico, is the ninth largest port in the country. Pleasure craft as well as many fishermen anchor here.

Tourists admire the waterfalls at Lake Buchanan, a highlight of the Vanishing Texas River Cruise.

The coastline of Texas along the Gulf of Mexico measures 367 miles. But if the shorelines of the bays, offshore islands, and rivermouths are included, it stretches for 3,359 miles. The major river is the Rio Grande, which forms the southern border, between Texas and Mexico. Other important rivers are the Pecos, Colorado, Guadalupe, Neches, Nueces, Brazos, Red, Sabine, San Antonio, and Trinity.

The climate of Texas varies widely from one end of the state to the other, with the coldest readings found in the northern Panhandle. There January temperatures average 35 degrees Fahrenheit, with a 76-degree-F. average in July. In southern Texas, warm, damp weather with temperatures of 60 degrees F. in January and 85 degrees F. in July is the norm. Eastern Texas has up to 46 inches of precipitation per year, while western Texas averages only 8 inches or less. Strong winds accompanied by sleet and rain can sweep across the state in winter, but snowfall occurs only in the north.

Horseback riding in Big Bend National Park, in the curve of the Rio Grande, brings visitors in direct contact with the desert lands of the American Southwest.

The History

Spanish conquistadors, commanded by Francisco Coronado, explored Texas in the 16th century, while searching for the famed Seven Cities of Cibola.

When the Spaniards arrived in what would become Texas in the 1500s, some 30,000 Indians were living in the region. In the east were the Caddo—farmers who lived in permanent dwellings. Some of them, including the Nacogdoches, Nasoni, and Neche tribes, formed a league called the Hasinai Confederacy. Along the coast were the Arkokisa, Attacapa, Katankawa, and other small tribes. Some of the Indians of Coahuila lived in the southern part of the region, adjacent to Mexico. In the plateaus to the west were the nomadic Lipan Apaches, and the north-central plains were hunting grounds for the Comanche and Tonkawa.

Just 27 years after Columbus discovered America, the Spanish began to explore Texas in the name of "glory, God, and gold"—mainly gold. In 1519 Alonzo Álvarez de Piñeda, who sailed from Jamaica, began to explore the Gulf Coast from Florida to Mexico, mapping it as he went. In 1528 another Spanish expedition was shipwrecked on the Texas coast. There were four survivors, one of whom, Álvar Núñez (called Cabeza de Vaca), led his companions on a trek among the Indians that lasted eight years and ended at a Spanish settlement near the Pacific Coast of New Spain (Mexico). There they told stories about Indian cities of great wealth in what is now the American Southwest.

Inspired by these tales, Francisco Vásquez de Coronado set off from Mexico in 1540 to look for the Seven Cities of Cibola—those fictitious realms of gold. With him was a Roman Catholic priest, Fray Juan de Padilla, the first Franciscan missionary to the region, who was later killed by the Indians whom he was trying to convert. The group passed through Texas in 1541 and reached the adobe dwellings of the Pueblo Indians farther west, but found no gold. Disappointed, Coronado gave up the search in 1542.

Hernando de Soto, the Spanish governor of Cuba, ventured from the west coast of Florida to what is now Oklahoma beginning in

1539. He died on the expedition, but some of his men pushed on into northeast Texas, reaching the vicinity of what is now Texarkana in 1542. Spain claimed the Texas area as a result of these explorations, and two missions were established by the Franciscans in 1682 near what is now El Paso.

The French entered the region in 1685, when Robert Cavelier (called La Salle) landed at Matagorda Bay and established a colony named Fort Saint Louis. This settlement was destroyed by the Indians two years later. But Spain was alarmed by the French presence, and sent new explorers and missionaries to strengthen its hold on the area. In 1690 a Franciscan friar traveling with the expedition of Alonso de León established the first mission in east Texas, San Francisco de los Tejas, along the Neches River.

By 1731 the Spanish had sent more than 90 expeditions into Texas. Many missions and forts were established, including the fort of San Antonio de Bexar, which was built to protect the mission of San Antonio de Valero. The settlement became the city of San Antonio. It was the seat of Spanish government in Texas from 1772 onward. Texas grew slowly because of its size and remoteness from Mexico City. More than 100 years after Spanish colonization began, the region had only about 7,000 settlers.

When the United States completed the Louisiana Purchase from France in 1803, it claimed that portion of Texas to which France had taken title during the 1600s. In 1819 the Adams-Onis Treaty with Spain gave the United States the rights only to a point bounded by the Sabine and Red Rivers.

When Mexico won its freedom from Spain in 1821, Texas was a part of the short-lived Empire of Mexico. Three years later Mexico became a republic, with Texas and Coahuila as one of its states. In 1820 a Missouri banker, Moses Austin, had asked Mexican officials to let him set up an American colony in Texas. The request was approved, but Austin died before he could organize the colony on the Brazos River. His son, Stephen F. Austin, brought 300 American families to Texas in 1821, and they established settlements at Washington-on-the-Brazos and Columbus, in southeastern Texas. In

1823 Austin laid out the settlement of San Felipe de Austin, in present-day Austin County, as the colonial seat of government. Mexico gave Austin additional land grants, and he expanded the boundaries of his colony.

Other Americans moved into Texas with the permission of the Mexican government; by 1830 Texas had a population of 25,000 settlers, most of them from the United States. But the Mexican government had become alarmed by the number of Americans in Texas, and conflict developed. In 1830 Mexico forbade further American immigration into Texas and the importation of slaves.

Mexican general Antonio López de Santa Anna became dictator-president of Mexico in 1833. He abolished the federal constitution and demanded personal control of state governments. In 1835 the American colonists in Texas revolted against Mexico. They had several battles with Mexican troops before their leaders met at San Felipe de Austin to organize a temporary government. The Texans formed a small army, and troops led by Colonel Benjamin Milam attacked San Antonio, taking control of the town on December 11, 1835. Santa Anna rushed north to put down the revolt with a large Mexican army. At San Antonio, a handful of American Texans, outnumbered 30 to 1, retreated into an old mission, the Alamo, to make a stand. Santa Anna's attack on the Alamo lasted from February 23 to March 6, 1836. The American garrison fought to the last man. All of the defenders, including Jim Bowie, Davy Crockett, and William B. Travis, were killed.

With the cry "Remember the Alamo!" Texas leaders met at Washington-on-the-Brazos and declared Texas independent of Mexico. David G. Burnet was chosen temporary president of the Republic of Texas, and Samuel Houston was made commander of the army. Santa Anna was still trying to put down the revolution. He had some 330 Texas prisoners shot to death in the town of Goliad, but the Texans continued to fight. In April 1836, Houston and his small army took Santa Anna's large army by surprise in the Battle of San Jacinto, defeating the superior force and capturing Santa Anna.

The best known historical site in Texas is the Alamo, the mission in San Antonio where a small force of 187 Texans was besieged by a large Mexican army in 1836.

Above:
Jim Bowie (1796–1836), a settler from Georgia, commanded the garrison at the Alamo. He invented the Bowie knife, a popular weapon used on the Western frontier.

At right:
The defenders of the Alamo included a former congressman from Tennessee, the frontiersman Davy Crockett (1786–1836), seen at right being bayoneted by a Mexican soldier.

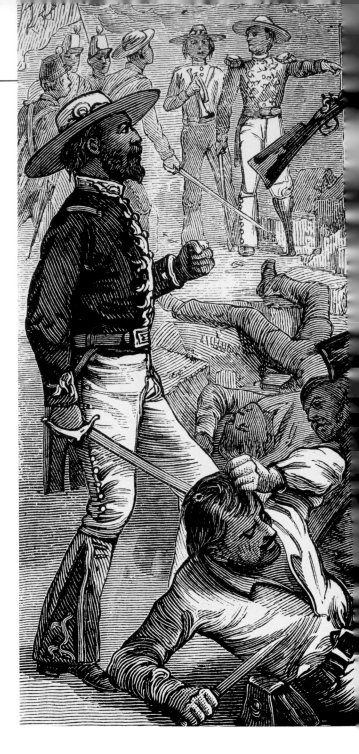

This victory ended the war and raised the republican flag, with its single star, over what would become the Lone Star State.

Sam Houston became the new president of the Republic of Texas, but many problems remained. The government had little money available, and parties of Mexicans continued sporadic raiding from across the disputed southern border. The obvious answer was to petition the United States for annexation, which the Republic did. However, European nations, especially France and Great Britain, wanted Texas to be independent so that the United States would not gain control of the Southwest. The Southern states wanted Texas in the Union because it was a slave-holding territory, but the North opposed the idea for the same reason. The Republic of Texas was not admitted to the Union for 10 years. In 1845 it became the 28th state.

When Texas was admitted to the Union, Mexico broke off diplomatic relations with the United States. Long-standing disputes over the Rio Grande border between Texas and Mexico were a major cause of the Mexican War, which began in 1846. Mexico surrendered in 1848, and gave up its claims to Texas, New Mexico, and California in the Treaty of Guadalupe Hidalgo.

Texas left the Union to join the Confederacy when the Civil War began in 1861. But the decision was not unanimous. Governor Samuel Houston, who had worked for union with the United States since 1838, refused to take an oath to support the Confederate States of America. He was put out of office and retired from public life.

More than 50,000 Texans fought for the Confederacy during the war, and the state sent huge quantities of food, textiles, and other goods to support the Southern cause. The Texas coast was blockaded by the Union Navy, which also occupied Galveston for a time. Although the Civil War ended on April 9, 1865, its last battle was fought on May 13 at Palmito Ranch, near the mouth of the Rio Grande, by soldiers who had not heard that the war was over.

The Reconstruction era that followed the Civil War brought occupation by federal troops and widespread racial violence incited by the Ku Klux Klan. After Texas was readmitted to the Union in

Sam Houston (1793–1863) commanded the Texans at the Battle of San Jacinto and later became the president of the Republic of Texas.

Galveston, which lies on a low island off the Gulf Coast, still contains many elaborate houses such as the Bishop's Palace, built in 1886.

1870, conflict decreased, and many new settlers moved in. Cattle ranching became a major industry, and large farmlands opened up along the railroad lines that crossed the state in the 1880s. Richard King extended the 75,000-acre tract he had bought in 1853 into the world's largest ranch—the 1.27-million-acre King Ranch, with some 40,000 cattle.

In 1900 a devastating hurricane struck the island city of Galveston, in the Gulf of Mexico, and killed some 6,000 residents in one of North America's worst natural disasters. The city was rebuilt into a major port for dry-cargo shipping. A year later, discovery of the Spindletop oil field near Beaumont signaled a new role for Texas as one of the nation's leading producers of oil and natural gas. Refineries and manufacturing plants were built, and coastal harbors were deepened to accommodate large ships that transported oil to world markets. When the United States entered World War I in 1917, many military training camps opened in the state.

In 1925 Texas became the second state, after Wyoming, to have a woman governor. She was Mrs. Miriam A. "Ma" Ferguson, who ran for office after her husband, Governor James E. Ferguson, was impeached. She was later elected to a second term.

During World War II, about 1,250,000 members of the armed forces trained in Texas. In 1947 the state suffered another major disaster when a French ship loaded with chemicals blew up in the harbor at Texas City. About 500 people were killed, 3,000 were injured, and the loss in property was about $70 million.

In 1973, NASA's Manned Spacecraft Center was renamed the Lyndon B. Johnson Space Center. This facility has made southeast Texas a center of space research and has attracted corporations that design and test space equipment.

To diversify the economy, manufacturing and other industries have expanded, but oil and petroleum are still vital to the Texas economy. Fluctuating oil prices directly affect the Texas economy and characterize their "boom and bust" economic cycle. Economic difficulties in the 1980s led to an increased state sales tax and budget cuts in health, welfare, and higher education.

The economy has stabilized and growth has resumed. Today Texas continues to expand its industries, with emphasis on cotton products such as clothing, machinery, and processed foods.

Education

Franciscan friars opened the first schools in Texas during the 1600s to teach farming techniques, spinning, and weaving to the

Houston is a major port for oil tankers, which reach the inland city by the 50-mile Ship Channel.

Once the center of the Texas cattle industry, Houston has grown to a major city since the discovery of oil.

Indians. During the period of Mexican rule, the government refused to set up schools with English-speaking teachers. But in 1854, nine years after statehood, a public-school system was established. The first library was organized in Austin by the Republic of Texas in 1839. Southwestern University (1840) was the first institution of higher education. When Texas became a state, there were two more—Mary Hardin-Baylor College and Baylor University, both

The NASA Lyndon B. Johnson Space Center near Houston has played a major part in the space program since the Mercury flights in the early 1960s. It is now the center of the shuttle program.

founded in 1845. By the turn of the century, Texas had 24 colleges and universities, including Austin College (1849), Saint Mary's University of San Antonio (1852), Trinity University (1869), Texas Agricultural & Mechanical University (1876), Texas Christian University (1873), Sam Houston State University (1879), Rice University (1912), and Southwest Texas State University (1899).

Mariachi bands, a tradition brought from Mexico, stroll along the Paseo del Rio in San Antonio.

The People

Almost 80 percent of the people in Texas live in metropolitan areas such as Houston and San Antonio. About 90 percent of them were born in the United States, and most of those who were born in foreign countries came from Mexico. The largest single religious group is the Roman Catholic. Other important denominations are the Baptists, Methodists, members of the Churches of Christ, Disciples of Christ, Presbyterians, and Episcopalians.

Below left:
The descendants of the German farmers who settled Fredericksburg in the 1840s celebrate Founder's Day.

Below:
The Tigua Indians, the oldest ethnic community in Texas, live on a Reservation near El Paso.

Famous People

Many famous people were born in the state of Texas. Here are a few:

Alvin Ailey 1931-1989, Rogers. Choreographer

Debbie Allen b. 1950, Houston. Entertainer

Lance Alworth b. 1940, Houston. Hall of Fame football player

Gene Autry b. 1907, near Tioga. Singing cowboy of movies

Ernie Banks b. 1931, Dallas. Hall of Fame baseball player

Robby Benson b. 1957, Dallas. Film actor: *Running Brave, Harry and Son*

Lloyd Bentsen b. 1921, Mission. Senate leader and Secretary of the Treasury

Raymond Berry b. 1933, Corpus Christi. Hall of Fame football player

Carol Burnett b. 1933, San Antonio. Five-time Emmy Award-winning television comedienne

Earl Campbell b. 1955, Tyler. Hall of Fame football player

Vikki Carr b. 1941, El Paso. Pop singer

Cyd Charisse b. 1921, Amarillo. Film dancer and actress: *Singin' in the Rain, Silk Stockings*

Claire Chennault 1890-1958, Commerce. World War II Air Force general

Ramsey Clark b. 1927, Dallas. U.S. attorney general

Tom Clark 1899-1977, Dallas. Supreme Court justice

Ornette Coleman b. 1930, Fort Worth. Jazz saxophonist

Joan Crawford 1904-77, San Antonio. Academy Award-winning actress: *Mildred Pierce, What Ever Happened to Baby Jane?*

Hugh R. Cullen 1881-1957, Denton County. Oil executive

Linda Darnell 1921-65, Dallas. Film actress: *Forever Amber, The Thirteenth Letter*

Mac Davis b. 1942, Lubbock. Country singer

Jimmy Dean b. 1928, Plainview. Country singer

James Frank Dobie 1888-1964, Live Oak City. Folklorist and educator

Sam Donaldson b. 1934, El Paso. Television newsman

Allen Drury b. 1918, Houston. Pulitzer Prize-winning novelist: *Advise and Consent, A Novel of Capitol Hill*

Sandy Duncan b. 1946, Henderson. Film actress: *Star Spangled Girl, The Cat from Outer Space*

Alvin Ailey founded one of the premier African-American dance companies in the country.

Lyndon B. Johnson, who became president after the assassination of President Kennedy in 1963, was instrumental in passing historic civil rights legislation and creating many Great Society programs for the underprivileged. At the end of his second term, Johnson retired to his ranch on the Pedernales River.

Shelley Duvall b. 1949, Houston. Film actress: *The Shining, Time Bandits*

Dwight D. Eisenhower 1890-1969, Denison. Thirty-fourth President of the United States

Dale Evans b. 1912, Uvalde. Cowboy film actress

James Farmer b. 1920, Marshall. Civil rights leader

Farrah Fawcett b. 1947, Corpus Christi. Film actress: *Logan's Run, The Cannonball Run*

Curt Flood b. 1938, Houston. Baseball player

George Foreman b. 1949, Marshall. Heavyweight boxing champion

A. J. Foyt b. 1935, Houston. Champion auto racer

"Mean" Joe Greene b. 1946, Temple. Hall of Fame football player

Larry Hagman b. 1931, Weatherford. Television actor: *I Dream of Jeannie, Dallas*

Najeeb Halaby b. 1915, Dallas. Airline executive

Patricia Highsmith b. 1921, Fort Worth. Novelist: *Strangers on a Train*

Ben Hogan b. 1912, Dublin. Champion golfer

Buddy Holly 1936-59, Lubbock. Rock singer

Rogers Hornsby 1896-1963, Winters. Hall of Fame baseball player

Johnny Horton 1929-60, Tyler. Country singer

Howard Hughes 1905-76, Houston. Airline and film executive

Gayle Hunnicutt b. 1943, Fort Worth. Film actress: *Scorpio; The Spiral Staircase*

Jack Johnson 1878-1946, Galveston. Heavyweight boxing champion

Lady Bird Johnson b. 1912, Karnack. Former first lady

Lyndon B. Johnson 1908-73, near Stonewall. Thirty-sixth President of the United States

Janis Joplin 1943-70, Port Arthur. Rock singer

Scott Joplin 1868-1917, Texarkana. Ragtime composer

Kris Kristofferson b. 1936, Brownsville. Film actor: *A Star Is Born, Semi-Tough*

Tom Landry b. 1924, Mission. Professional football coach

Bob Lilly b. 1939, Olney. Hall of Fame football player

Joshua Logan 1908-88, Texarkana. Broadway producer and director: *Mister Roberts; South Pacific*

Barbara Mandrell b. 1948, Houston. Country singer

Mary Martin 1913-90, Weatherford. Stage actress: *The Sound of Music, Peter Pan*

Steve Martin b. 1945, Waco. Comedian and actor

Eddie Mathews b. 1931, Texarkana. Hall of Fame baseball player

Don Meredith b. 1938, Mount Vernon. Football player

Spanky McFarland 1928-91, Fort Worth. Star of the *Little Rascals* comedies

Ann Miller b. 1919, Chireno. Film actress and dancer: *On the Town, Kiss Me Kate*

Roger Miller 1936-92, Fort Worth. Country singer

C. Wright Mills 1916-62, Waco. Sociologist

Joe Morgan b. 1943, Bonham. Hall of Fame baseball player

Audie Murphy 1924-71, near Kingston. Film actor: *To Hell and Back, The Red Badge of Courage*

Byron Nelson b. 1912, near Fort Worth. Champion golfer

Chester W. Nimitz 1885-1966, Fredericksburg. World War II admiral

Roy Orbison 1936-88, Wink. Rock singer

Buck Owens b. 1929, Sherman. Country singer

Fess Parker b. 1926, Fort Worth. Film actor: *Davy Crockett, King of the Wild Frontier; Old Yeller*

As a Navy admiral during World War II, Chester W. Nimitz initiated the Central Pacific offensive in 1943.

Valerie Perrine b. 1943, Galveston. Film actress: *Lenny, Slaughterhouse Five*

Katherine Anne Porter 1890-1980, Indian Creek. Author: *Ship of Fools; Collected Stories of Katherine Anne Porter*

Wiley Post 1898-1935, near Grand Saline. Aviation pioneer

Paula Prentiss b. 1939, San Antonio. Film actress: *Catch-22, The Stepford Wives*

Ray Price b. 1926, Perryville. Country singer

Dan Rather b. 1931, Wharton. Television news anchorman

Rex Reed b. 1938, Fort Worth. Film critic

Debbie Reynolds b. 1932, El Paso. Film actress: *Singin' in the Rain, The Unsinkable Molly Brown*

Tex Ritter 1907-74, near Murvaul. Cowboy film actor

Frank Robinson b. 1935, Beaumont. Hall of Fame baseball player

Nolan Ryan b. 1947, Refugio. Baseball pitcher

Ann Sheridan 1915-67, Denton. Film actress: *King's Row, The Man Who Came to Dinner*

Willie Shoemaker b. 1931, Fabens. Champion jockey

Jaclyn Smith b. 1947, Houston. Television actress: *Charlie's Angels*

Liz Smith b. 1923, Fort Worth. Newspaper columnist

Terry Southern b. 1928, Alvarado. Screenwriter: *The Loved One, Easy Rider*

New York Giants' quarterback Y.A. Tittle led the league in passing in 1963, throwing for 36 touchdowns and 3,145 yards.

Sissy Spacek b. 1949, Quitman. Academy Award-winning actress: *Coal Miner's Daughter, Crimes of the Heart*

Tris Speaker 1888-1958, Hubbard. Hall of Fame baseball player

Sly Stone b. 1944, Dallas. Rock singer

Jack Teagarden 1905-64, Vernon. Jazz trombonist

Y. A. Tittle b. 1926, Marshall. Hall of Fame football player

Rip Torn b. 1931, Temple. Film actor: *Sweet Bird of Youth, Heartland*

Lee Trevino b. 1939, Dallas. Champion golfer

Tommy Tune b. 1939, Wichita Falls. Broadway choreographer

Walton H. Walker 1899-1950, Belton. World War II general

Barry White b. 1944, Galveston. Soul singer

Kathy Whitworth b. 1939, Monahans. Champion golfer

Robert W. Wilson b. 1936, Houston. Nobel Prize-winning physicist

Babe Zaharias 1914-56, Port Arthur. Champion golfer

Colleges and Universities
There are many colleges and universities in Texas. Here are the more prominent, with their locations, dates of founding, and enrollments.

Abilene Christian University, Abilene, 1906, 3,457

Austin College, Sherman, 1849, 1,135

Baylor University, Waco, 1845, 10,421

East Texas State University, Commerce, 1889, 5,485

Hardin-Simmons University, Abilene, 1891, 1,802

Howard Payne University, Brownwood, 1889, 1,427

Incarnate Word College, San Antonio, 1881, 2,282

Lamar University, Beaumont, 1923, 11,295

McMurry College, Abilene, 1923, 1,518

Midwestern State University, Wichita Falls, 1922, 5,056

Our Lady of the Lake University of San Antonio, San Antonio, 1911, 2,112

Prairie View A&M University, Prairie View, 1876, 4,937

Rice University, Houston, 1912, 2,604

St. Edward's University, Austin, 1876, 2,631

St. Mary's University of San Antonio, San Antonio, 1852, 2,595

Sam Houston State University, Huntsville, 1879, 10,837

Southern Methodist University, Dallas, 1910, 5,288

Southwest Texas State University, San Marcos, 1899, 18,497

Southwestern University, Georgetown, 1840, 1,204

Stephen F. Austin State University, Nacogdoches, 1917, 1,295

Sul Ross State University, Alpine, 1920, 1,863

Texas A&I University, Kingsville, 1925, 5,302

Texas A&M University, College Station, 1876, 33,479

Texas Christian University, Fort Worth, 1873, 5,692

Texas Lutheran College, Seguin, 1891, 1,072

Texas Tech University, Lubbock, 1923, 19,611

Texas Wesleyan University, Fort Worth, 1890, 1,493

Texas Women's University, Denton, 1901, 5,610

Trinity University, San Antonio, 1869, 2,281

University of Houston of Clear Lake, Houston, 1971, 3,556; *of Downtown*, Houston, 1974, 8,702; *of Victoria*, Victoria, 1973, 1,223

University of Texas at

Arlington, Arlington, 1895, 20,404; *at Austin*, Austin, 1883, 35,911; *at Dallas*, Richardson, 1969, 4,841; *at El Paso*, El Paso, 1913, 14,599; *at San Antonio*, San Antonio, 1969, 14,663; *at Tyler*, Tyler, 1971, 2,509; *of the Permian Basin*, Odessa, 1969, 1,476

Wayland Baptist University, Plainview, 1908, 921

West Texas State University, Canyon, 1909, 5,146

Where To Get More Information
Tourism Division
Texas Department of Commerce
Box 12728
Austin, TX 78711
Or Call 1-800-8888-TEX

Further Reading

General

Aylesworth, Thomas G. and Virginia L. Aylesworth. *America's Southwest*. New York: Gallery Books, 1986.

Aylesworth, Thomas G. and Virginia L. Aylesworth. *State Reports: The Southwest: Colorado, New Mexico & Texas*. New York: Chelsea House, 1992.

Colorado

Carpenter, Allan. *Colorado*, rev. ed. Chicago: Childrens Press, 1978.

Casewit, Curtis, W. *Colorado*. New York: Viking, 1973.

Downey, Matthew T., and F. T. Metcalf. *Colorado: Crossroads of the West*. Boulder, CO: Pruett, 1976.

Fradin, Dennis B. *From Sea to Shining Sea: Colorado*. Chicago: Childrens Press, 1993.

Kent, Deborah. *America the Beautiful: Colorado*. Chicago: Childrens Press, 1989.

Schmidt, Cynthia. *Colorado: Grassroots*. Phoenix, AZ: Cloud Publishing, 1984.

Sprague, Marshall. *Colorado: A Bicentennial History*. New York: Norton, 1976.

Sprague, Marshall. *Colorado: A History*. New York: Norton, 1984.

Ubbelohde, Carl E., and others. *A Colorado History*. rev. ed. Boulder, CO: Pruett, 1982.

New Mexico

Beck, Warren A. *New Mexico: A History of Four Centuries*. Norman, OK: University of Oklahoma Press, 1982.

Carpenter, Allan. *New Mexico*. rev. ed. Chicago: Childrens Press, 1978.

Fergusson, Erna. *New Mexico*. rev. ed. New York: Knopf, 1964.

Fradin, Dennis B., and Judith B. Fradin. *From Sea to Shining Sea: New Mexico*. Chicago: Childrens Press, 1993.

Jenkins, Myra E., and A. H. Schroeder. *A Brief History of New Mexico*. Albuquerque, NM: University of New Mexico Press, 1981.

Murphy, Dan. *New Mexico, the Distant Land: An Illustrated History*. Northbridge, CA: Windsor Publications, 1985.

Reeve, Frank D. and A. A. Cleaveland. *New Mexico: Land of Many Cultures*, rev. ed. Boulder, CO: Pruett, 1980.

Simmons, Marc. *New Mexico: A Bicentennial History*. New York: Norton, 1977.

Stein, R. Conrad. *America the Beautiful: New Mexico*. Chicago: Childrens Press, 1988.

Texas

Carpenter, Allan. *Texas*, rev. ed. Chicago: Childrens Press, 1979.

Connor, Seymour V. *Texas: A History*. Arlington Heights, IL: AHM, 1971.

Fradin, Dennis B. *From Sea to Shining Sea: Texas*. Chicago: Childrens Press, 1992.

Frantz, J. B. *Texas: A Bicentennial History*. New York: Norton, 1976.

Frantz, Joe B. *Texas: A History*. New York: Norton, 1984.

Richardson, Rupert N., and others. *Texas: The Lone Star State*. 4th ed. Englewood Cliffs, NJ: Prentice-Hall, 1981.

Stein, R. Conrad. *America the Beautiful: Texas*. Chicago: Childrens Press, 1989.

Picture Credits

Courtesy of Alvin Ailey American Dance Theater/Eric N. Hong: p. 88; Courtesy of Albuquerque Convention and Visitors Bureau/Ron Behrman: pp. 37, 40; Courtesy of Albuquerque Convention and Visitors Bureau/Dick Kent: p. 36; Courtesy of Colorado Tourism Board: pp. 15, 16; Courtesy of Colorado Tourism Board/Russ Finley: p. 13; Courtesy of Colorado Tourism Board/Ron Ruhoff: pp. 19, 20; Courtesy of Colorado Tourism Board/Rod Walker: p. 17 (right); Culver: pp. 6, 24, 47, 74, 77, 78, 79; Courtesy of Denver Metro Convention and Visitors Bureau: p. 11; O. C. Garza: p. 72; Jeff Gnass: p. 3 (top); Courtesy of Greeley, Colorado Office of Cultural Affairs: p. 12; Jill Heisler: pp. 3 (bottom), 21, 42, 46; Michael Murphy: pp. 54, 86; Courtesy of National Park Service/Fred E. Mang, Jr.: pp. 8-9, 35; National Portrait Gallery: pp. 81, 89; Courtesy of New Mexico Economic and Tourism Department/Mark Nohl: pp. 31, 32-33, 38, 39, 41, 43, 45, 48, 50; Courtesy of New Mexico State Records Center and Archives: p. 29; Courtesy of New York Giants: p. 92; New York Public Library: pp. 22-23; Courtesy of Office of U.S. Senator Pete Domenici: p. 52; Richard Reynolds: pp. 71, 73, 82, 84, 85, 87; Courtesy of Special Collections Department, Nimitz Library, U.S. Naval Academy: p. 91; Courtesy of State of Colorado Design Center: pp. 5, 9; Courtesy of Texas Department of Highways and Public Transportation: pp. 56-57, 59, 60, 61, 62, 63, 64, 65, 67; Courtesy of Texas Office of the Governor: p. 53; Tourism Division, Texas Department of Commerce: p. 4; U.S. Air Force: p. 17 (left); Wide World: pp. 27, 51.

Cover photos courtesy of Colorado Tourism Board/Ron Ruhoff; New Mexico Economic and Tourism Department/Mark Nohl; and Richard Reynolds.